The Opening of the Maritime Fur Trade at Bering Strait

Key words: fur trade, maritime fur trade, North Pacific Ocean history, Alaska history, Hawaii history, Russian American Company, Bering Strait Region, Arctic, Alaska Eskimos, Chukchi.

Transactions
of the
American Philosophical Society
Held at Philadelphia
For Promoting Useful Knowledge
Volume 95, Pt. 1

The Opening of the Maritime Fur Trade at Bering Strait

Americans and Russians Meet the *Kaŋiġmiut* in Kotzebue Sound

John R. Bockstoce

American Philosophical Society
Philadelphia ◆ 2005

ISBN: 0-87169-951-
US ISSN: 0065-9746

Library of Congress Cataloging-in-Publication Data

Bockstoce, John R.
The opening of the maritime fur trade at Bering Strait: Americans and Russians meet the *Kaŋiġmiut* in Kotzebue Sound / John R. Bockstoce.
p. cm. – (Transactions of the American Philosophical Society, ISSN 0065-9746 ; v. 95, pt. 1)
Includes bibliographical references and index.
ISBN-13: 978-0-87169-951-0 (pbk.)
ISBN-10: 0-87169-951-6 (pbk.)
1. Fur trade–Alaska–History–19th century. 2. Alaska–Commerce–Russia–History– 19th century. 3. Russia–Commerce–Alaska–History–19th century. 4. Russia–Commerce–United States–History–19th century. 5. United States–Commerce–Russia–History– 19th century. 6. Merchant ships–Alaska–History–19th century. 7. Merchant ships–Russia–History–19th century. 8. Astor, John Jacob, 1763-1848. I. Title. II. Series.
HD9944.U46A43 2005
382'.45685–dc22

2005043570

Design and Typesetting
Boyd Printing Co.

For Ernest S. Burch, Jr.

Contents

Preface

THE MARITIME FUR TRADE WAS AN IMPORTANT COMMERCIAL FORCE IN THE Bering Strait region from the early nineteenth century until the outbreak of the Second World War; nevertheless, its origins are not well understood. But two important documents—which have received little scholarly attention—shed considerable light on the genesis of this trade. These manuscripts describe the voyages of the American trading brigs *General San Martín*[1] in 1819 and *Pedler*[2] in 1820, and they provide valuable information on the complicated relationships that existed between the American maritime traders and the Russian officials in Kamchatka and Alaska, as well as with the inhabitants of the Bering Strait region in the first quarter of the nineteenth century.

[1]Eliab Grimes MS.
[2]John Walters MS.

ACKNOWLEDGMENTS

I WISH TO THANK DR. KATHERINE ARNDT, PROFESSOR WILLIAM BARR, Dr. Ernest S. Burch, Jr., Dr. Philip Cronenwett, Commander Andrew David, Dr. Norman Fiering, Ms. P. W. Fox, Professor John Hattendorf, Dr. Mary Malloy, and Professor José Amor y Vázquez for commenting on drafts of this manuscript. I am also grateful to Dr. Michael LaCombe for his assistance with the Astor papers and to Ms. Susan Danforth for her help with the Arrowsmith charts and in obtaining illustrations. Mr. Brian Walsh and Ms. Patricia Lai generously helped in securing printed and manuscript materials. Alice and Will Thiede of Carto-Graphics drew the maps. Mary McDonald helpfully and ably saw the manuscript through to publication.

I am also grateful to the Hawaii State Archives and to the Historical Society of Dauphin County, Pennsylvania, for permission to quote from their manuscripts and to the John Carter Brown Library at Brown University and the Beinecke Rare Book and Manuscript Library of Yale University for permission to reproduce illustrations.

List of Illustrations

List of Maps

The Opening of the Maritime Fur Trade at Bering Strait

Introduction

The arrival of the first fur trading vessels at Bering Strait was the result of adventures that began in the eighteenth century. Although Russians had been exporting furs from Alaska to Siberia for more than thirty years,[3] the origin of a trans-Pacific trade can be dated to Captain James Cook's third voyage of exploration. In 1779 Cook's men were astonished to discover that the sea otter pelts they had acquired for trifles from the Indians on the Northwest Coast of North America fetched phenomenal sums from the merchants of Canton,[4] and when accounts of this trade appeared in print in the 1780s, they set off an entrepreneurial rush to the Northwest Coast.

For the Americans in particular, John Ledyard's unauthorized report, published in Hartford, Connecticut, in 1783, was a powerful lure to enter the maritime fur trade.[5] Previously, American merchants in East Asia had been obstructed by the East India Company's monopoly, but after the colonies had achieved independence, this constraint no longer applied to American vessels. Ledyard's account of skins "which did not cost the purchaser sixpence sterling [on the Northwest Coast] sold in China for 100 dollars"[6] drew New England merchants to a new enterprise at a time when Great Britain, in the aftermath of the War of Independence, was embargoing the products of the American whale and cod fisheries.[7] To the Americans' advantage, however, the East India Company's monopoly also hampered other British traders, and from about 1790 onward American ships dominated the maritime fur trade via highly lucrative triangular voyages from Boston, to the Northwest Coast, to Canton, and return.

Nevertheless, by 1810 the boom years were in the past. Sea otter skins were in shorter supply, hence more expensive, and President Thomas Jefferson's Embargo Act of 1807—an effort to keep the United States out of the war between Britain and France—had prevented

[3] Black 2004:59–72.

[4] Today, Guangzhou. Cook and King 1784, III:437.

[5] Gibson 1976:3–5, 1992:22—23; Malloy 1998:24–25.

[6] Ledyard 1783:70.

[7] Lower 1978:34–35.

American vessels from sailing for foreign ports. "How Congress failed to throw out this absurdity is a mystery," wrote Paul Johnson. "While American ships remained in harbor, their crews idle and unpaid, smuggling flourished and British ships had a monopoly of legitimate trade."[8] To make matters worse, the War of 1812 brought both a British blockade of the United States' ports and the capture of American merchantmen.

With the end of hostilities in 1815, however, the Americans returned to the trade in force, while simultaneously their voyages to the Pacific took on new dimensions and destinations in the search for profits. Sea otters, and later, beavers, were only two of the fur bearers' skins acquired from the Northwest Coast Indians and traded to China. American ships also began carrying cargoes from Russian America to China, and they now traded throughout the entire Pacific for a wide variety of commodities: betel nut, sugar, bird nests, *bêche de mer* (trepang), sandalwood, "and anything else that would catch an eye and open a purse in Canton."[9]

"The vessels were on the alert to add any other venture that gave a reasonable prospect of a saving voyage," wrote F. W. Howay. "It followed that the ship owner could do no more than indicate in a general way the conduct to be pursued by the master. So much depended upon the conditions prevailing when the vessel reached the coast or other place at which she was to call. The result was that the maritime fur-trade had become, as one ship-owner expressed it, "a voyage of adventure."[10]

[8]Johnson 1997:256.
[9]Gibson 1992:252.
[10]Howay 1973:105.

Chapter 1

The Voyage of the General San Martín (1819)

At the same time, the emerging political revolutions against the rule of Spain in South America created new opportunities for trade with that continent. In 1817, as a stepping stone to an attack on the Viceroyalty of Peru, an Argentine general, José de San Martín, crossed the Andes "in one of those supreme feats of war"[11] and defeated a Spanish army — an act which led to Chile's independence and the opening of her ports to foreign shipping. American merchant vessels, some of which had hitherto been involved in smuggling in Chile, soon began to visit her ports to take on cargoes of copper for the China trade.

John Jacob Astor of New York, the central figure in the American fur trade, had entered the Pacific trade at the very beginning of the nineteenth century. Astor often seized new opportunities as soon as, or sooner than, his competitors. Shortly after Chile's liberation, a fleet of American vessels, including the *Enterprise*, owned by Astor, sailed there from Hawaii, reaching Coquimbo in early 1818. In command of the *Enterprise* was Captain John Ebbets, Astor's trusted agent and associate. At Coquimbo Ebbets took on a load of copper; during the visit, he also purchased a ship for William Heath Davis and Thomas Meek, who may have acted as surrogates for Astor and perhaps another trading company as well. She was a brig, the *General San Martín* (150 tons, 4 cannon),[12] a prize that had been captured by a revolutionary privateer.[13]

Davis had arrived in Chile in command of the ship *Eagle*, which was owned by the Boston firm of Boardman and Pope. Boardman and Pope ships often cooperated in Pacific trading ventures with Astor's vessels. While the fleet was in Chile, Thomas Meek took command of the *Eagle* from Davis. Eliab Grimes, a widely experienced mariner and trans-Pacific trader, became captain of the *General San Martín*. The *Enterprise* and the *General San Martín* then departed for Hawaii.[14]

---

[11]Collier and Sater 1996:37.

[12]Vagin 1872:73; Pierce 1990:399–400. I am grateful to Dr. Katherine Arndt for translations of many of the Russian passages quoted herein.

[13]Howay 1973:150.

[14]Porter 1932:280; Pierce 1976:232-233.

In September 1818, the *General San Martín* touched at Okhotsk, the Siberian trading settlement on the northwest coast of the Okhotsk Sea. Okhotsk lay at the terminus of the land route across Asia from St. Petersburg and was the transshipment port for the Russian American colony. Failing to find a buyer for his cargo at Okhotsk, after waiting only two days, Grimes headed for Petropavlovsk, on the east coast of the Kamchatka Peninsula. There, on behalf of Astor and Boardman and Pope, he sold Peter Dobell 25,000 rubles' worth of trade goods, which Dobell then loaded aboard Astor's brig *Sylph* for shipment to Manila. Grimes then took aboard another of Astor's captains, William J. Pigot,[15] with a consignment of 60,649 of Astor's fur seal skins, which for three years Pigot had been unable to sell. Nevertheless, during that period of time, Pigot had kept Astor appraised of the potential of the Siberian trade. The *General San Martín* sailed for Hawaii in October 1818.[16]

Ebbets, Davis, Meek, Grimes, Pigot, and a few others made up a loose commercial fraternity of Pacific Ocean merchant mariners. This group of experienced Northwest Coast traders and entrepreneurs operated throughout the Pacific in the early years of the nineteenth century. They acted not only as agents and captains for several American trading companies but also, as opportunities arose, owned trading vessels by themselves or in partnership with those companies and with one another. Eliab Grimes, for instance, was an agent for Astor and several other firms, including Boardman and Pope, and Marshall and Wildes of Boston.[17]

But peerless among them in entrepreneurial energy was Peter Dobell, who led several of them into an attempt to create a whaling operation in Kamchatka to help feed the population there. Dobell was an Irish-American who, after serving as an Indian fighter in western Pennsylvania, went to sea and eventually landed in China in 1798 and spent seven or more years in

[15]William J. Pigot was probably related to John Ebbets by marriage (Porter 1932:261, 274).

[16]Porter 1931:654; Vagin 1872:73–75; Howay 1973:96; Pigot to John Jacob Astor, January 7, 1816, and October 26, 1818, John Jacob Astor Collection, Baker Library, Harvard Business School, Boston, Massachusetts.

[17]Pierce 1990:132, 399–400; Malloy 1998:83, 97, 100–101; Howay 1973:119–121, 150; Porter 1931:676, 680; Kotzebue 1821b:2:195, 198, 203.

the Canton area. There, in 1805, he assisted Captain Ivan Fedorovich Kruzenshtern during the round-the-world voyage of the Russian ship *Nadezhda (Hope)* and consequently established a relationship with the Russians in eastern Asia. Much later he learned of a severe shortage of supplies in Kamchatka, and in 1812 sailed to Petropavlovsk with two ships loaded with provisions. He traveled aboard one of them, John Jacob Astor's brig *Sylph*, and stayed in Kamchatka. Dobell then traveled throughout the region, seeing firsthand its poverty and its potential.[18]

Provisions were always a problem for the Russians in those regions. In fact, almost as soon as they achieved their remarkably swift conquest of northern Asia and parts of Alaska, they faced the critical difficulty of supplying food to their own people. In particular, "on the Okhotsk Seaboard and the Kamchatka Peninsula," James R. Gibson wrote, "the Russians were beset with a chronic question of how, in such a harsh and distant region, to provision not only fur traders but also state servitors, missionaries, convicts, serfs, and scientific expeditions." For example, despite government efforts to encourage farming in Kamchatka, the experiment was a failure,[19] and not only was state aid insufficient to sustain the population, but the catches of fish and animals were continuously poor.[20] In 1817, consequently, Captain of the First Rank Petr Ivanovich Rikord, a capable and honest naval officer who had recently been appointed as the commandant of Kamchatka, was forced to consider any opportunities available to him to acquire food and provisions.

The year before, in 1816, Dobell, "the tireless promoter,"[21] had proposed a plan to the Governor-General of Siberia, Ivan Pestel', to supply foodstuffs to Kamchatka from the Philippine Islands, and Pestel' had directed Rikord to discuss the matter with Dobell. Previously Dobell had traveled to St. Petersburg, where he became a subject of the Tsar, and had arranged to be

---

[18]Dobell I:314-316, II:121; Pierce 1990:271—273; Wenger 1984:26—27; Tikhmenev 1978:87, 125–128.

[19]Gibson 1969:211–212; Beechey 1831:238–239, 524–529.

[20]Vagin 1872:39.

[21]Pierce 1990:400.

appointed both as a Court Councilor and as the Russian Consul General in Manila. The Spaniards, however, did not accept his credentials, and in 1818 he returned to Petropavlovsk, Kamchatka, where, with his trading business there in disarray, he "pestered" his friend Rikord with a plan to create a whaling operation as a way of providing meat for the indigenous population.[22]

Dobell must have sent word of his proposal to his associates in Hawaii, because on June 16, 1819, the *General San Martín*, with Eliab Grimes in command, arrived for the second time in Petropavlovsk. Dobell purchased the cargo, part of which he kept at Petropavlovsk, another part he sent to Okhotsk, and the rest he intended to sell in Manila.[23] Aboard the *General San Martín* was William J. Pigot, as well as a crew for the *Sylph*, which, under Pigot's command, was to sail at once for Manila with Dobell aboard.

Pigot also carried with him powers of attorney from William Heath Davis, John Ebbets, and Thomas Meek, and he concluded a contract, collectively, for them and for himself —with Rikord and Dobell signing for the Russian government, subject to the Tsar's confirmation— to have exclusive rights to conduct a whale fishery for ten years, beginning in 1821, "on the eastern shores of Siberia." In return Pigot and his associates were to sell their whale products to the Russians and to instruct a number of Russian sailors in the methods and conduct of the whale fishery.[24]

Rikord unfortunately had an enemy in Aleksandr Nikolaev, the Russian American Company's resident agent in Petropavlovsk. "Both at that time and later, the trade of foreigners in Kamchatka and their protector, Rikord, were under strict supervision of the company's agents," wrote the historian V. Vagin. "Its Kamchatkan commissioner, Nikolaev, reported to the board of

[22]Vagin 1872:61–62.

[23]Vagin 1872:75. All Russian dates have been converted to the Gregorian calendar. The Julian calendar date, used in Russia, was June 4.

[24]Vagin 1872:425–427, 441–443; Frank Golder Collection, Hoover Institution on War, Revolution and Peace, Stanford, California, Box No. 14, Folder 7, Dobell 1812–29 IV-5, No. 4, Dobell to Nesselrode, February 1, 1819.

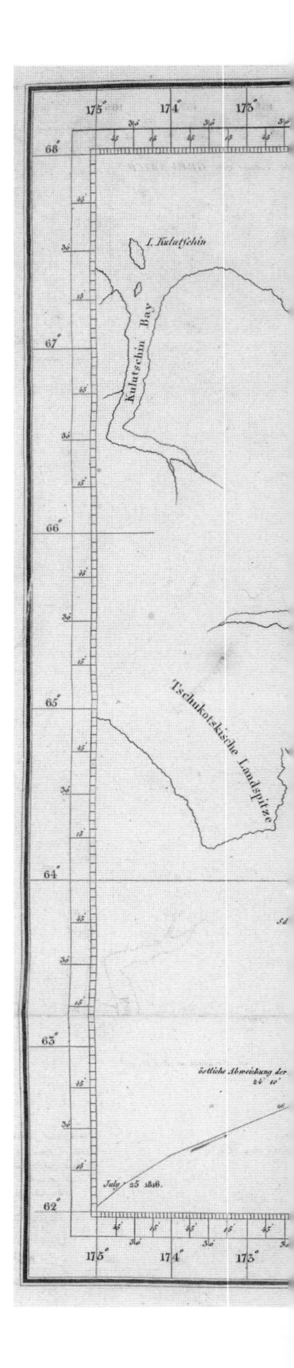

175°
174°
173°
68°
67°
66°
65°
64°
63°
62°
I. Kulatschin
Kulatschin Bay
Tschukotskische Landspitze
östliche Abweichung der
24° 10'
July 25 1816.

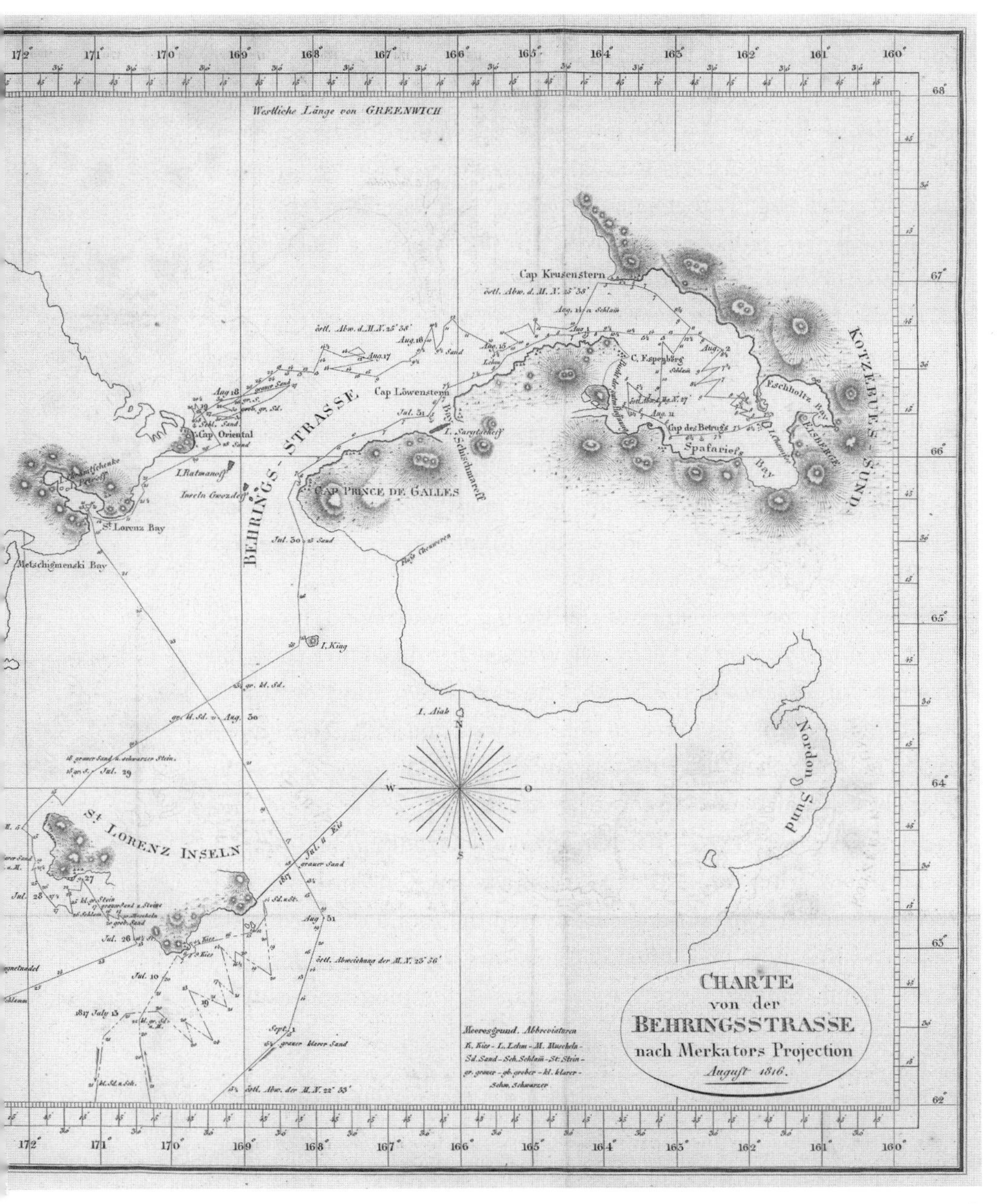

Map 1. Kotzebue's Chart of the Bering Strait Region. From Otto von Kotzebue, *Entdeckungs-Reise in die Sud-See und nach der Berings-Strasse.* Credit: John Carter Brown Library at Brown University.

directors in all detail not only the actions but sometimes even the words of Rikord and the foreigners. In Kamchatka he was completely justifiably called a spy. . . ."[25]

Although Rikord had acted in the interest of the welfare of the people of Kamchatka, in St. Petersburg the Russian American Company's directors immediately attacked the arrangement, seeing it as a dangerous infringement on the company's monopoly in its territories, which included all of Kamchatka, most of the Kurile Islands, and the shores of the Okhotsk Sea, as well as much of present-day Alaska. The Company protested that this group of foreigners would use the whaling operation as a cover for hunting sea otters and fur seals, among other prohibited activities.[26] In St. Petersburg the government bowed to this pressure and nullified the contract, but because of the immense distance (more than 8,000 miles of overland travel) and slow communications (about six months, one way) between St. Petersburg and the East Asian settlements, Rikord, as we shall see, did not receive this order until September 1820.[27]

Most importantly for the history of the Bering Strait region, however, the *General San Martín*'s visit to Petropavlovsk was her departure point for a commercial reconnaissance in the North. The idea of searching for furs at Bering Strait had probably occurred to John Ebbets and his associates in Hawaii in 1817. In October, the Russian naval officer Otto von Kotzebue reached Honolulu aboard the 180-ton brig *Riurik* during his round-the-world voyage of discovery (1815—1818). Kotzebue's expedition had probed the waters north of Bering Strait and, in an area where Captain Cook had not closed with the American shore, he discovered the sound that bears his name. There the Russians encountered numerous aggressive Eskimos.[28] The explorers found that the Eskimos were expert, cunning traders who

[25]Vagin 1872:79.

[26]Dmytryshyn et al. 1989:329–330.

[27]Vagin 1872:64–68, 75—84, 86; Tikhmenev 1978:126–128, 463–465(19); Golder 1917:16, 17, 39, 105, 107, 111, 113.

[28]For simplicity and clarity, in this essay I use the term "Eskimo" to refer to both the Iñupiat (the inhabitants of the Seward Peninsula and northern Alaska) and Yup'ik (the inhabitants of southwestern Alaska, Saint Lawrence Island, and the easternmost shores of the Chukchi Peninsula).

possessed many furs, which, the Russians correctly assumed, were destined to be traded to the Chukchi on the west shore of Bering Strait, at the northeastern extremity of Asia.[29]

At that time Russians were unpopular in Hawaii because of a clumsy intrusion into Hawaiian politics, which included an attempted land-grab by a German employee of the Russian American Company.[30] Despite this unpleasantness, in Honolulu Kotzebue proved to be a skillful diplomat, and he and his officers got on particularly well with the American traders William Heath Davis, John Ebbets, and Thomas Meek, among others. In fact, the Americans sent their ships' boats to help tow the *Riurik* out of the harbor on her departure.[31] Because of their good relations, it is highly likely that the Russians told the Americans about their discoveries in the North — and in December 1817, Ebbets, Davis, Meek, and others left Hawaii for Chile, where, as we have seen, Ebbets bought the brig *General San Martín*. In fact, the *General San Martín* may have been purchased specifically to carry out a reconnaissance based on Kotzebue's discoveries: Sometime before her arctic voyage of 1819, her owners entered into an agreement with the King of Hawaii to sell her for 2500 piculs of sandalwood on her return from the North.[32]

Kotzebue's expedition was sponsored by Count Nikolai Petrovich Rumiantsev, the Chancellor of Russia, who, at his own expense, had sent it in search of a northwest passage—a northern water route between the Pacific and Atlantic oceans.[33] In any case, on August 15, 1818, the *Riurik* ended her voyage and anchored off Rumiantsev's palace in the river Neva.[34] There can be little doubt that Kotzebue reported his discoveries to his

---

[29]Kotzebue 1821b, 1:209-211, 228-229.

[30]Chamisso 1986:xvii–xviii; Pierce 1965; 1990:445–446; Daws 1968:51–52.

[31]Kotzebue 1821a 2:116; 1821b, 2:195, 198, 203; Chamisso 1874:206—207; 1986:191–192; Barratt 1988:155–156, footnote 2.

[32]Eliab Grimes Business Letter Book, Grimes to John Ebbetts, September 21, 1819. I am grateful to Dr. Ernest S. Burch, Jr. for bringing this document to my attention. A picul was a Chinese measure of mass equal to 133 1/3 pounds.

[33]Barratt 1988:19–25; Pierce 1990:435–436.

[34]Kotzebue 1821a:2:148; 1821b:2:287.

patron then. Not long after that, judging from Grimes' correspondence, Rumiantsev must have written to Rikord in Kamchatka, suggesting further research on Kotzebue's discoveries at Bering Strait.[35]

During the *General San Martín*'s visit to Petropavlovsk in 1818, it is likely that Grimes discussed with Rikord the possibility of a voyage to Bering Strait. In 1819 Rikord, having received Rumiantsev's request for further investigations, no doubt viewed the *General San Martín*'s planned northern voyage expediently: It was a convenient means of using an existing venture, which, at no cost to the Russians, could be harnessed to help confirm Kotzebue's surveys for Rumiantsev.[36] In fact, to assist the expedition Rikord not only gave Grimes a copy of Kotzebue's chart of the Bering Strait region, but also provided him with an interpreter to help in communicating with the natives there.

In Petropavlovsk on June 29, 1819, "After gitting the necessaries ready," Grimes wrote, "at 2 pm Capt Ricord very politely set me onboard, after passing a little time took his leave[,] wishing me a prosperous voyage. . ."[.][37] The *General San Martín* then weighed anchor and stood out of the bay, pausing briefly to allow Grimes to receive a letter from Thomas Meek[38] from a Russian brig, inbound from Novo-Arkhangel'sk, the Russian American Company's headquarters on the Northwest Coast.[39]

Five days later, on the fourth of July, Grimes wrote, "this being a remarkable day[,] the people was [?regaled] with fresh pork and an extra glass of grogg."[40] But with Kotzebue's report of the aggressive natives at Bering Strait no doubt in mind, the next day he began preparing for the encounter. "We lost no time in gitting ready to meet any hostile intentions from natives," Grimes wrote. "Should we meet with any [we] put our large guns in order and muskets[,] making cartridges."[41]

[35]Eliab Grimes Business Letter Book, Grimes to Rikord, December 15, 1819.

[36]Based on other analyses of Russian accounts, in earlier publications (Bockstoce 1977:6—7; 1988:2) I incorrectly identified Grimes as "Gray."

[37]Eliab Grimes, journal, *General San Martin*, June 29, 1819, in Eliab Grimes Business Letter Book.

[38]Grimes journal., June 30, 1819.

[39]Novo-Arkhangel'sk is today Sitka, Alaska.

[40]Grimes journal, July 4, 1819.

[41]Grimes journal, July 5, 1819.

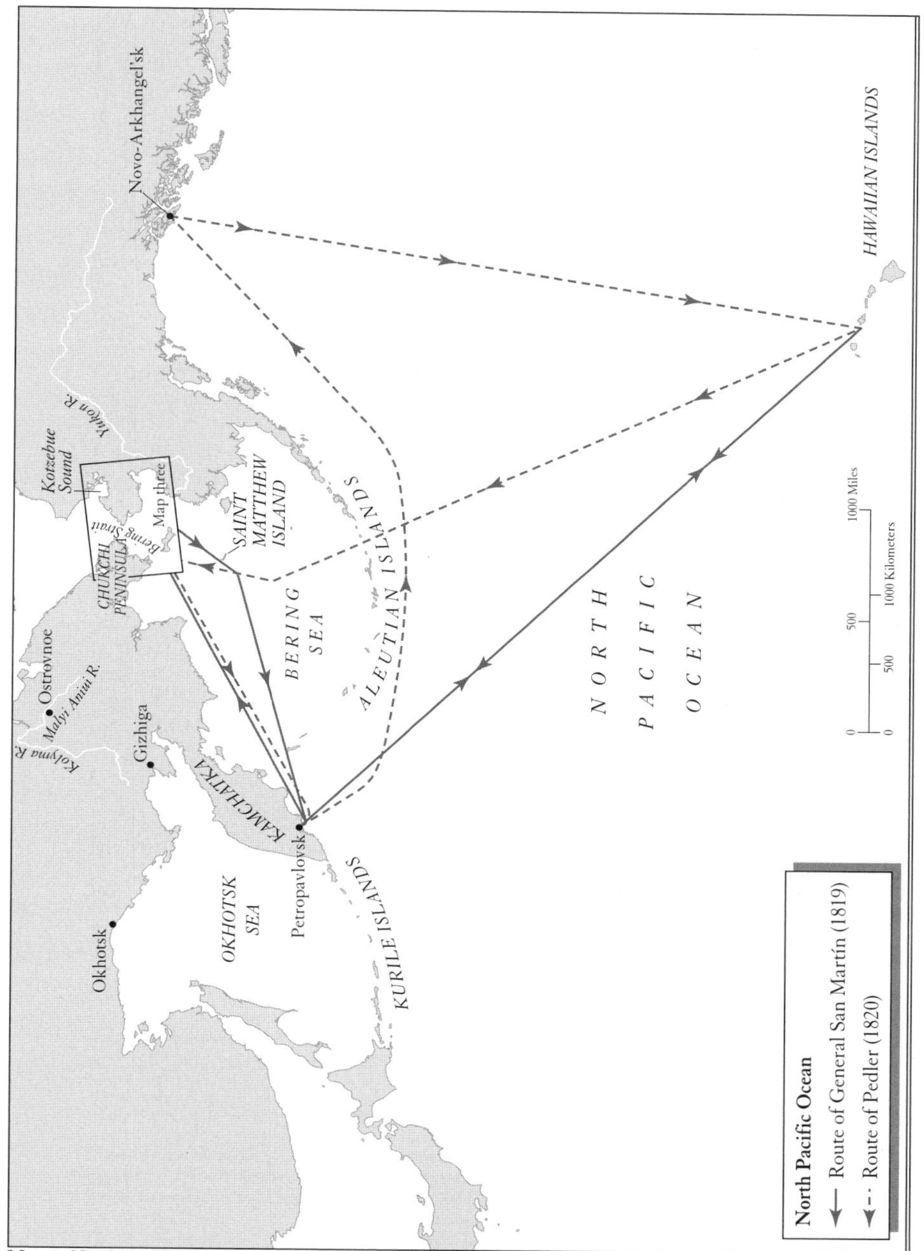

Map 2. North Pacific Ocean. Routes of the *General San Martín* (1819) and *Pedler* (1820).

Grimes continued on a northeasterly course, parallel to the Asian coast.[42] On the eleventh, in thick fog, the *General San Martín* reached the northwest corner of Saint Lawrence Island and hove to where Kotzebue had paused.[43] Grimes sent his boat to shore and an hour later it returned accompanied by several native umiaqs.[44]

"When along side," he wrote, "I found they had a considerable quantity of horse teeth [walrus tusks][45] and a few fox skins which we bought for a little tobacco." The Eskimos left when night approached, but the following day twelve umiaqs arrived with twelve to fourteen persons in each boat. "We bought what they had for sale," Grimes continued, "which in all amounted to about forty skins and about thirty hundred weight[46] of teeth[.] I bicame quite elated with the good success I had met with which led me to believe I should make a good voyage."

"You might naturally ask the reason I did not continue about the Island longer," he wrote to John Ebbets in September. "I was anxious to git the fur and teeth at the Bay of St. Lawrence and its neighbouring places before they were carried to the Russian settlements[,] and having been presented one of Kotzebues chart of his sound and Chesmurofs [Shishmaref's] straits[47] by Capt Ricord and strongly recommended to visit the place as it would be the most likely to reward me for my labour while the season was favorable."

So Grimes, prompted by Rikord and aided by a copy of Kotzebue's chart, headed first to Saint Lawrence Bay[48] on the eastern coast of the Chukchi Peninsula. After three days at anchor, the word of the brig's presence had

---

42Grimes journal, July 7, 1819.

43Kotzebue 1821b I:195-196; Grimes to John Ebbets, September 21, 1819, Eliab Grimes Business Letter Book. I have inserted paragraph indentations throughout the text of the letter. This was the settlement of Sivuqaq; today, Gambell, Alaska.

44An umiaq is a large open-framed Eskimo boat, the hull of which is formed by a covering of hides. The Saint Lawrence Island Eskimos covered their boats with walrus hides.

45"Sea horse" (walrus) tusks.

46Grimes bought more than 3,300 pounds of walrus ivory. A hundredweight (*cwt.*) is equal to 112 avoirdupois pounds, or approximately 50.8 kg.

47Grimes' "Chesmurofs straits" is Shishmaref Inlet, the embayment on the north coast of the Seward Peninsula (66°15´N., 166°05´W.) about halfway between Bering Strait and Kotzebue Sound. Otto von Kotzebue thought it might have potential as a waterway to the interior and named it after his lieutenant, Gleb Semenovich Shishmarev (Kotzebue 1821b:199—203; Orth 1967:867).

48Today, Zaliv Lavrentia, Chukotka.

Illustration 1. Eskimos of Saint Lawrence Island, 1816. From Louis Choris, Voyage *Pittoresque Autour du Monde*. Credit: private collection.

spread, and "there were great numbers alongside[,] however I found there was no one had fur or teeth of any consequence except the chief and his brother and in order to trade I was requested to go ashore."

Whether "the chief and his brother" had accumulated trade goods on their own account or whether they were acting as trading masters for the local population is not clear. "I must confess the invitation was not so pleasing as it would have been for New York or Boston," he continued, "however during my stay I was treated very well and after examining their property it was sent on board after agreeing and paying them which was forty skins of the same bulk of tobacco moderately stowed into the same bag which contained the skins."

Grimes then headed directly to the Diomede Islands, two pillars of rock that stand midway in Bering Strait, about twenty miles from either shore. There he quickly learned the central reality of commerce in that region. He discovered that a robust and well-organized intercontinental native trade existed between America and Asia and that its participants did not welcome foreign competition. "I fell in with two of the Tschutski [Chukchi] chiefs with an hundred men each which comes from the East cape[49] of the Asiatic coast yearly and makes this Island called Imjacklima ["Big Diomede Island"][50] there [sic] central place of trade and receiving all the fur near Cape Prince of wales[51] and as far to the southward as Norton Sound. . ."

Thus it appeared to Grimes that "Big Diomede Island" served as an *entrepôt* between the Eskimos of Alaska and the Chukchi of northeasternmost Asia. "After spending four or five days with them and not being able to do any thing for want of proper trade I left for and [sic] Island about twenty miles to the NNW[.]"

Kotzebue's chart of Bering Strait shows another island (which does not exist), northwest of the two Diomedes and their neighbor, Fairway Rock. I believe that Grimes, aided by a copy of Kotzebue's chart, thought he was heading for this island, when in fact he was heading for East Cape (Mys Dezhneva). The bold headland of East Cape, the eastern promontory of Asia, is joined to the Chukchi Peninsula by a twenty-mile-wide lowland. From a distance it appears to be an island. To judge from his course when leaving the Diomedes, I assume that Grimes headed to East Cape, where the Chukchi traders, more than 200 strong, again blocked his attempt to intercept the furs.

"I had no sooner arrived than I saw the whole fleet to the number of eighteen boats carrying twelve and thirteen men each following in order to prevent my trading[,] as they had done at the one I had just left[.] finding myself foiled in this I bore up and passed through Bering Straits."

As Grimes approached his next anchorage, Shishmaref Inlet, he may well have had in mind Kotzebue's report of his encounter there with the Eskimos and readied his crew for action.[52]

"On the 27 July fell in with Chesmerofs straits [Shishmaref Inlet]. . . having a large village on the western shore and not seeing any natives I con-

[49]East Cape, the easternmost point of Asia, was named by Captain James Cook. In 1898 it was officially renamed Mys Dezhneva (Cape Dezhnev), honoring Semen Dezhnev, who, in 1648, led the first party of foreigners to reach it.

[50]*Imaqłiq*, "Big Diomede Island," is Ostrov Ratmanova, Russia.

[51]Cape Prince of Wales, also named by Captain Cook, is the westernmost point of continental North America.

[52]Kotzebue 1821b I:204.

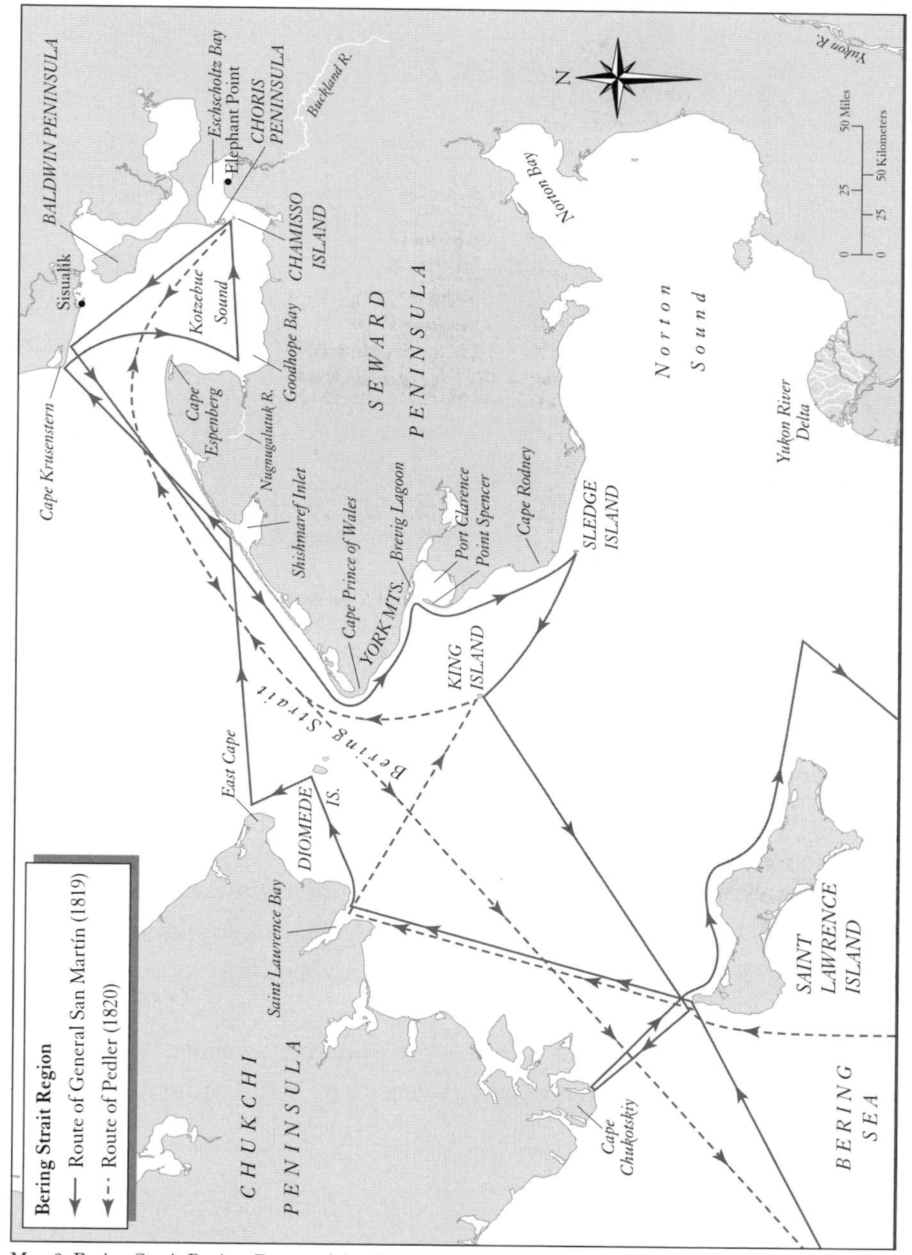

Map 3. Bering Strait Region. Routes of the *General San Martín* (1819) and *Pedler* (1820). Credit: Carto Graphics.

Illustration 2. A Chukchi coastal summer camp, probably at Saint Lawrence Bay, 1828. Frederick Lütké, *Voyage Autour du Monde*. Credit: private collection.

cluded they were curing their winter stock of fish[.] on the 29th I left for Kotzebues Sound and on the 30th we made Cape Cruzenstern [Krusenstern] [,] the northern point latitude 67°10[53] where we saw a few natives but owing to the heavy surf were not able to land, I stood for the southern shore and in the evening came to an anchor [in] 4½ fathoms water . . . our distance from shore fourteen to fifteen miles b[e]aring from west to SE." The *General San Martín* was anchored in Goodhope Bay, the southwestern embayment of Kotzebue Sound.

"The following morning I sent Mr. Dyrkee[54] to examine the shoers so far as was practicable[.] he returned after being twenty four hours without see-

[53]His latitude is accurate within two nautical miles. Cape Krusenstern is officially placed at 67°08′N. (Orth 1967:546).

[54]Mr. "Dyrkee" [Durkee] was probably the mate of the *General San Martín*. Mr. Durkee was, perhaps, Thomas Durkee, a merchant mariner who operated out of Hawaii at that time (see, for instance, William J. Pigot and John Meek, contract with George Tamoree, June 23, 1820, State Archives of Hawai'i, Honolulu).

Illustration 3. Interior of a Chukchi house in Saint Lawrence Bay, 1816 or 1817. Credit: Ludovik Choris drawings, Western Americana Collection, Beinecke Rare Book and Manuscript Library, Yale University.

ing any natives[.] I than made sail for the head of the sound keeping the northern shore in view but did not see any natives untill we arrived at the head[,] where we fell in with about one hundred and fifty of them[.]"[55]

The *General San Martín* was probably now near the Choris Peninsula and Chamisso Island, where Kotzebue had anchored in 1816, in the inner waters of Kotzebue Sound. This area was within the boundaries of the Buckland River Eskimos, the *Kaŋiġmiut*, one of approximately thirty nations of indigenous peoples in northwestern Alaska.[56] It is most likely that

[55]Eliab Grimes to John Ebbets.

At that time the North Magnetic Pole was located in the vicinity of the Boothia Peninsula in Arctic Canada. Because of the considerable magnetic variation from true north, in Kotzebue Sound Grimes' "northern shore" was probably the coast of today's Baldwin Peninsula.

[56]Burch 1998a:203, 259–278.

Under the term *northwestern Alaska* I include the lands lying west of a line from Norton Bay, on the Bering Sea, to the Colville River delta, on the Beaufort Sea. This area includes the Seward Peninsula and about half of northern Alaska, which roughly coincides with the territories of the Iñupiaq-speaking Eskimo nations.

Illustration 4. Eskimos of Kotzebue Sound, 1816. From Louis Choris, *Voyage Pittoresque Autour du Monde*. Credit: private collection.

Grimes encountered the Eskimos near Elephant Point[57] in Eschscholtz Bay, where the *Kaŋiġmiut* gathered to hunt the great numbers of belukha[58] whales that enter the estuary each summer.[59]

"I bought eighty skins," Grimes continued," but no [walrus] teeth[60] except three small ones which they esteemed much more valuable than their skins, for pointing their spears and using them as a pick ax. . .[.] I found they had the Russian long knife and large blue bead also a small piece of iron about [word omitted] inches long stub answering for an adz. . .[.]"

There Grimes confirmed two things that Kotzebue had learned: that the trade goods possessed by the Eskimos came from Asia and that glass beads

[57]Elephant Point was so named in 1826 by the British explorer Frederick William Beechey because of the frozen remains of mammoths that were found eroding from its bluff (Beechey 1831:232).

[58]These white whales *(Delphinapterus leucas)*, ten- to fifteen-feet long and approximately 3000 pounds at maturity, were formerly called *beluga whales.*

[59]Burch 1998a:273–277.

[60]Walruses *(Odobenus rosmarus)* are not usually found in Kotzebue Sound.

Illustration 5. An Eskimo man in Kotzebue Sound, 1816.
Credit: Ludovik Choris drawings, Western Americana Collection, Beinecke Rare Book and Manuscript Library, Yale University.

and iron were in demand. Grimes then headed on, in search of more trading opportunities. "I left this keeping the southern shore in sight and when we ware about half way to the entrance[61][,] came to in four fathoms[.] sent Mr. Durkee in the direction SW where hee saw a few natives that were a fishing[.] they not having any fur nor seeing any other[,] he shortly returned."

Grimes added a note to Ebbets about the depth of water and the low, tundra-covered shores surrounding inner Kotzebue Sound and about the advantage of having a small boat—which he had aboard the *General San*

[61]The entrance to Kotzebue Sound. Grimes is probably referring to Cape Espenberg.

Martín—to approach the coast: "the situation of the sound is such and from that to Cape Prince of Wales in regard to shoal water making off to such a distance . . .[requiring] a tender to examine where we were hardly able to see the shores which are low[,] the land in the country rising to a moderate hight entirely destitute of shrub or tree."

"On the 9th of August anchored of Cape Cruzenstern abrest of a Village when we were visited by a number of natives[.] finding they had no fur or teeth I left for Chesmerofs straits and arrived on the eleventh[,] where we saw a number of natives and bought what skins they had[,] which was about twenty but no teeth and have every reason to believe they seldom or ever see any of the sea horses [walruses] in the sound or about the shores north of the Cape[.]"

The reason that Grimes was unable to buy any furs at Cape Krusenstern, and only a few at Shishmaref Inlet, may have been that the Eskimos had just returned from their great annual trade fair at *Sisualik*,[62] the sandspit in the northeastern corner of Kotzebue Sound. More than 1700 persons from most of the Eskimo nations of northwestern Alaska (as well as a few Indians and Chukchis) met there annually—in a season of truce—to trade, dance, feast, and engage in athletic competitions, among other activities.[63] It is possible that most of the furs had been exchanged by then and, in fact, may already have been on their way to the Chukchi Peninsula when Grimes had stopped at "Big Diomede."

"I left here with a fresh gale from NW[,] thick weather[,] and passed Prince of Wales during the night. . .brought in a little to the southward of Cape Prince of Wales[.] in the afternoon it became more moderate with pleasant weather[.] stood to south there[,] keeping near the shore but saw no natives nor the appearance of any as it is barren and mountainous[,] rising abruptly from the waters edge until you get to the latt 65°22[,] where it trends to the E by S[.]"[64]

62Today, Sheshalik.

63Burch 1998b:151–162.

64Grimes had sailed along the face of the York Mountains.

Illustration 6. Men of Shishmaref Inlet, 1816.
Credit: Ludovik Choris drawings, Western Americana Collection, Beinecke Rare Book and Manuscript Library, Yale University.

Grimes continued his reconnaissance along the southwestern coast of what is today the Seward Peninsula. He wrote, "after running about thirty miles[,] came to[.] in the morning I found we had anchored near a fine beach covered with driftwood[.][65] on landing we saw some natives which informed me by signs they had been with their boats and sold their fur[,] pointing to the north of west[.][66] a few miles to the south by east I found a good har-

[65]The *General San Martín* probably lay off the beach that encloses Brevig Lagoon.
[66]They pointed toward Bering Strait.

bour[.] although formed by low land[,] it [is] of a sufficient hight to keep the sea off[.]"

Grimes had found the large, sheltered embayment of Port Clarence, which is enclosed by Point Spencer's long gravel spit. Another important native trade fair, similar to the one at *Sisualik* in Kotzebue Sound, took place on the Point Spencer sandspit. Here members of more southerly Eskimo nations, from as far south as the Yukon River delta, met annually with King Islanders, Diomeders, Seward Peninsula Eskimos, Asiatic Eskimos, and Chukchis.[67]

"I left this and examined the shores [as] far as Cape Rodney and Sledge Island and all the natives we saw informed me the same as before mentioned. I found it to correspond exactly to what the Tchutski chiefs had informed me [—] that they get most of their fur from the Americans[.]"[68]

"Finding I was not able to do anything in this quarter I run for Kings Island and arrived on the 18th of August[.] here I bought. . .a hundred skins[,] , thirty of them silver grey [foxes] and half of thoes we had to buy with the boat [the *General San Martín*'s longboat] anchored near the shore[,] owing to a fresh breeze which [?raising] a short sea"[.]

The fact that the King Island Eskimos possessed so many furs indicates that they were traders themselves. The only local fur products available at King Island (a tall, vertical-sided speck of rock, nearly forty miles off the coast of the Seward Peninsula) were from seals, polar bears, and, occasionally, arctic foxes.

Grimes then warned Ebbets of another reality of trading with the Eskimos of the Bering Strait region. Referring to the steep swell —and, by extension, to its accompanying breakers— that he encountered at King Island, he explained, "when [heavy surf] is the case the natives will not visit you, and to trade with them on shore you run a great risque of your boat and people being captured[,] as they have made two attempts and it will always

[67]Burch 1998b:162–163; Ray 1964:75.

[68]Unlike western Alaska, the Chukchi Peninsula yields comparatively few furs (Schweitzer and Golovko 1995:19—22).

be found difficult to trade in thoes seas for want of a harbour where they can visit you with ease and you then feel yourself safe on board[,] trading the usual way with natives"[.] Grimes was presumably drawing on his experiences in trading with the Indians on the Northwest Coast, where traders had always to be on their guard in case of hostile action and consequently trading usually took place aboard ship.

Judging from Grimes' reference to two attempts by the Eskimos to capture his longboat and crew, I suspect that the *General San Martín's* men may have had difficult encounters with the Eskimos in Kotzebue Sound and at King Island. This is not surprising. In 1816, when the *Riurik* was on the west side of Bering Strait at Saint Lawrence Bay, Otto von Kotzebue learned from a Chukchi man there that Eskimos on the east side of the strait had a reputation for treachery. "The Tschukutskoi live in eternal enmity with the [Eskimos]; and my venerable guest, without hesitation, declared them all to be bad men. As a proof of his assertion, he said, that they behaved friendly as long as they considered themselves weaker; but robbed and murdered strangers without hesitation, if they were strong enough, and were able to do it without danger; and, for this reason he thought they wore knives in their sleeves, and use their wives to entice them."[69]

Grimes continued his report. "I left here for Clark's Island [Saint Lawrence Island] and on my arrival at the Village where I sailed first[70] the chief informed me that the Tchutska traders from Cape Anadyr[71] had been to the island during my absence and bought all there was[,] both teeth and fur of any size[,] as they all know where to meet the traders[,] which is at the NW part of the Island[.] I amediately left in hopes to fall in with them and on the 22nd arrived at the cape[,] where I fell in with a number of natives[72][.] they inform me the traders had arrived and that they had sold

[69]Kotzebue 1821b I:262.

[70]The settlement of *Sivuqaq*; today, Gambell, Alaska.

[71]Cape Anadyr does not exist on modern maps, although it did appear as the southeasternmost promontory of the Chukchi Peninsula on some Russian maps of the eighteenth century (Efimov 1964:55, 74). I believe that Grimes is referring to Cape Chukotskiy. Lying near the southeast point of the Chukchi Peninsula, it is the closest point of continental land to Saint Lawrence Island.

[72]The *General San Martín* may have been at the settlement of *Qiighwaq (Kivak)*, near Cape Chukotskiy (Hughes 1984:248).

them their fur and teeth and had mounted their raindeer and were on there way to the Russian settlements[73][.] (I forgot to observe that I had a linguist which was through the [word omitted] of Capt Ricord) however I got about thirty teeth that had lately been taken and about four hundred weight of whalebone"[.][74]

Grimes then spent two days unsuccessfully trying to find a harbor nearby on the Chukchi Peninsula, where he hoped to buy reindeer meat from the natives, but he finally gave up and returned to Saint Lawrence Island to conduct further explorations.[75] At the northeastern corner of the island he learned from the natives that they also had already sold all their "furs and teeth" to the traders. "I was now convinced," he added, that "there was nothing more to be done to advantage on the north. . . ." So, on August 28 he headed south. After searching for "Preobragenia" Island, a nonexistent island that his Arrowsmith chart indicated to be southwest of Saint Matthew Island,[76] on the ninth of September the *General San Martín* reached Petropavlovsk again. There Grimes immediately wrote his long report to John Ebbets in New York.[77]

Ebbets—who, as we have seen, had bought the *General San Martín* in Chile in 1818—arrived in New York in September 1819, still in command of

[73]Grimes was referring to Russian trading centers at the head of the Sea of Okhotsk and near the lower Kolyma River. The Russian trade fair at Ostrovnoe on the Malyi Aniui, a tributary of the Kolyma, 800 miles west of Bering Strait, was founded in 1789 (Ray 1992:98). It took place for several days in the spring (Cochrane 1824, I:311–324).

[74]*Whalebone* is baleen, the keratinous plates that grow from the upper jaw of baleen whales and with which they filter plankton from the water. Baleen, because of its flexibility and durability, was highly sought for manufacture into corset stays, among many other uses (Bockstoce 1986:208, 220, 353). This baleen most likely was taken from a bowhead whale (*Balaena mysticetus*).

[75]Saint Lawrence Island was named by Vitus Bering in 1728. In addition to a copy of Kotzebue's map, Grimes also carried a chart of the Bering Strait region that was based on Captain Cook's surveys. On Cook's chart of Bering Strait (Cook and King 1784, II:between 466 and 467) there are four islands: "Saint Lawrence Island," which is in fact the northwestern tip of Saint Lawrence Island, and two "Clerke's Islands." Grimes found that all three islands were part of "Clark's Island." Grimes also found that a fourth island, "Anderson's Island," east of Clerke's Islands, did not exist.

[76]Aaron Arrowsmith published a nine-sheet atlas of charts of the Pacific Ocean in 1798, with corrections in 1810 and 1814. The charts were widely used by mariners in the early nineteenth century. The version that Grimes was using indicated an island, "Preobragenia [Transfiguration] of the Russians Charts," a substantial island lying southwest of Saint Matthew Island. The information about this island may have originated from the charts that resulted from Ivan Syndt's voyage of 1764 (Black 2004:80; Hayes 2001:80, map 115), one of which was published in London in 1780 (Coxe 1780: between 300 and 301). I am grateful to Andrew David and Susan Danforth and the John Carter Brown Library for their assistance and information regarding Arrowsmith's charts.

[77]Grimes to Ebbets.

John Jacob Astor's ship *Enterprise*. There he concluded a four-year voyage during which he had traveled throughout the Pacific, carrying cargoes of sea otter and seal skins, sandalwood, and copper to Canton.[78] But Ebbets learned on his arrival that John Jacob Astor had departed from New York in June for extended travels in Europe, leaving the conduct of his business affairs in the capable hands of his son, William Backhouse Astor.[79] Ebbets no doubt informed the younger Astor of Eliab Grimes' activities in the Pacific in 1818 and of his plans for a northern cruise in 1819.

Grimes continued his letter of September 9, 1819, to Ebbets with succinct advice about the Bering Strait trade. "In attempting to carry on a trade in thoes seas the vessel should arrive by the first of July or before[,] if the ice will admit[.] collect all that can be got at Clarks Island[,] touch at Cape Anadyr and St. Lawrence Bay[,] proceed to the island in the straits[80][,] where you may stand a chance of getting a part of the fur that comes from the American coast [,] but not all untill they are tought to believe that a vessel will visit them yearly[,] as they all know at what time to meet the traders[,] and the whole business is all over by the first or tenth of august[.] the[y] amideately leave this for the East Cape and from that to the Russians settlements on the river Kovima[81] and Ingiga[82] at the head of ochotska sea[,] where they dispose of their fur. . ."

Thus Grimes had confirmed Kotzebue's observation[83] and identified for Ebbets the great flow of furs that annually were carried west, out of Alaska and across Bering Strait, to the Russian trading centers. Furthermore, he suggested a means of intercepting the furs by encouraging the Eskimos to anticipate annual visits by trading vessels.

He then listed the trade goods that the natives sought: "[They] receive in return large knives from 18 to 24 inches long and one fourth of an inch

[78]Howay 1973:114; Malloy 1998:100–101; Ogden 1941:79.

[79]Porter 1931:1163–1164.

[80]"Big Diomede Island."

[81]See footnote 73. As we have seen, this was the annual trade rendezvous that took place at Ostrovnoe on the Malyi Aniui River, a tributary of the Kolyma.

[82]Probably Gizhiga, founded in 1753 on the north shore of the Sea of Okhotsk (Armstrong 1965:55).

[83]Kotzebue 1821b I:209–211, 228–229.

thick[,] ornamented with brass near the Handle[,] also a lance in the form of a spontoon[84] having a bar on each side similar to that of an . . .Index on a Quadrant inlaid with brass, large scissors, small adzes, hatchets, iron pots, copper tea kettles, looking glasses, sewing needles, large blue & dark glass beads, size of a nutmeg[,] sheet lead & the best Cazan[85] Tobacco[.]"

Grimes' instructions must have directed him to examine the potential amount of walrus ivory and fur seal skins that might be available in the Bering Strait region. He first corrected a misconception about walruses shedding their tusks: "The idea of finding Sea Horse teeth about these shores is equally absurd as that of finding guineas in the streets of New York — or that they shed their teeth any oftener than a Bullock does his horns, as has been mentioned by some[,] is equally erroneous, as I have bought them standing in the upper part of the head [,] weighing from 1 to 8 pounds[,] the size of the head in proportion to that of the teeth as the small ones belong to the younger animals."[86]

Then Grimes turned to the question of fur seals. "I can with safety inform you there is no fur Seal[87] in any place or Island that I have visited[,] which is all to the Northward of Clark's[,] including the one in Kotzebues Sound."

Continuing his report, Grimes tallied the results of his barter: "I have subjoined a list of fur & teeth, & what I gave[:] 226 Red Foxes, 34 Silver

[84]Grimes is referring to an espontoon (halberd), a weapon, the distal end of which was a blade with transverse stops at the base. The blade was mounted on a pike pole. Halberds were used in Russia from the beginning of the seventeenth century, and their blades often contained inlaid metallic ornamentation. These weapons also reached the Bering Strait Eskimos (Bockstoce 1977:70).

[85]Kazan' is a city on the Volga River, a former fur trade center in Tatarstan, a region of southern Russia where tobacco is grown. Kazan' was the capital of the Khanate of Sibir, which Ivan IV ("The Terrible") captured in 1552, thus beginning the founding of the Russian Empire (Armstrong 1965:14; Lantzeff and Pierce 1973:66–72).

[86]The idea that walrus ivory could be collected on the shores of Bering Strait probably originated with the reports of Semen Dezhnev's expedition to East Cape and the Anadyr' River. Dezhnev and his men discovered a walrus rookery near the mouth of the Anadyr' and collected a quantity of walrus ivory there in the years after his voyage of 1648. Nevertheless, the report of his voyage remained obscure, in a Yakutsk archive, until Gerhard Frederich Müller, a scientific participant in Vitus Bering's second expedition, came upon it and published it. The report received widespread attention in the English speaking world when William Coxe (1780:313–320) described Dezhnev's voyage (Fisher 1981:4-8, 37, and passim).

[87]Although fur seals *(Callorhinus ursinus)* are occasionally found in the Bering Strait region, their primary range is in the central and southern Bering Sea and throughout the northern North Pacific.

Grey,[88] 32 White, 17 Blue,[89] 3 Black, 85 Martin skins,[90] 10 pack same 19 each, 9 Small beavers,[91] 1 land Otter,[92] 1 Cat Skin,[93] 66 Muskrats,[94] & 1 kind I am not acquainted with but is said to be of Value[95] & should say from 2 1/2 to 3 tons of Horse teeth[.]

For these Grimes payed "145 large knives[,] 30 of those belonging to yourself[,] a pr Old Pistols, 5 Looking Glasses, 1 carp[enter]s Adze[,] 1 Hammer, 1 Pick Axe, 3 Iron pots, 11 of those Iron Kettles from the Sultan,[96] 4 lb of those small blue Beads, & about 3 poods[97] of Cazan Tobacco that I got of Mr. Dobell, shirt & 1 pr trousers. . ."[98]

Elsewhere in his business letter book Grimes noted, apparently to aid his memory, the "trade for the tschutkus[.]" He listed "large thick knives from 10 to 20 inches in llength[,] from 1 1/2 eight to 2 [?eighths] of an inch thick on the back, 1 1/2 inch wide, kazan tobacco, flints & steels,[99] lead, scissors — iron pots, sewing needles, round blue and read [sic] beads about the size of large buck shot[.] black [beads of the same size][,] looking glasses[,] dark & light sky blue beads size of a nutmeg[,] and of prunes & cast in the form of this [a cylindrical bead is indicated] made of glass [—] some white[,] best of cazan tobacco[,] a few pick axes[,] knives 3 feet long[,] lances about a foot long with a bar in the center projecting 1 1/2 [?]eight

[88]Red, silver, black, and cross foxes are color phases of the red fox (Vulpes vulpes), which live in most parts of Alaska.

[89]White and blue foxes are color phases of the arctic fox (Alopex lagopus). Arctic foxes are found throughout most of the Bering Sea's and Arctic Ocean's coasts and far out on sea ice as well.

[90]The American marten *(Martes americana)* is a New World relative of the Eurasian sable. Martens inhabit coniferous forests.

[91]The American beaver *(Castor canadensis)* lives in most of the forested areas of mainland of Alaska.

[92]The northern river otter *(Lutra canadensis)* is found throughout sub-arctic Alaska.

[93]Probably a lynx *(Lynx canadensis)*. Lynx are primarily forest dwellers.

[94]Muskrats *(Ondatra zibethicus)* inhabit lakes, rivers, and swamps throughout sub-arctic Alaska.

[95]Possibly a wolverine *(Gulo gulo)*. Wolverines are found throughout mainland Alaska.

[96]The *Sultan* was owned by Boardman and Pope of Boston. Her first voyage to the Pacific took place between 1815 and, probably, 1819. In early 1818 she had been in Chile, where Captain Isaac Whittemore was taken aboard, ill, as a passenger. Whittemore died aboard her and "was put in a Hogshead of Rum, that he might be preserved until we could reach the Land." He was buried in the Marquesas Islands (Malloy 1998:158).

[97]A pood, or pud, was a Russian measure of mass equal to 36.11 pounds avoirdupois (approximately 16.38 kg). Grimes acquired the tobacco in Petropavlovsk.

[98]Grimes to Ebbets.

[99]For igniting fires.

each side[,][100] iron pots holding from 4 to 5 gallons[,] small axes and adzes. . ."[101]

Grimes estimated that a trading cruise to the Bering Strait region could be carried out as a segment of a more comprehensive voyage to the North Pacific: "A voyage to the North connected with business at this place[102] or with a North West Voyage[103] as it would not take more than 2 1/2 [months] I should think might answer. . . . I think there might be about $10,000 worth of fur & teeth collected for $1,000 of trade."[104]

Most importantly, however, the northern cruise of the *General San Martín* had produced a valuable cargo of commercial intelligence. Grimes had learned that furs and walrus ivory from coastal and interior Alaska were carried westward by the Eskimos to the vicinity of Bering Strait. There they were bartered to Chukchi traders—who also visited Saint Lawrence Island—in return for knives, pots and other metal goods, beads, and tobacco. The Chukchi then carried the furs farther, to trade with Russians on the Kolyma River and at the head of the Sea of Okhotsk. But Grimes also learned that two valuable commodities he almost certainly sought for the Chinese market were more difficult to acquire: He discovered that fur seal skins were not available in the Bering Strait region and that walrus ivory did not litter the shores, waiting to be collected.

In Petropavlovsk Grimes reported the details of his cruise to Petr Rikord and agreed to continue the Bering Strait survey for Rikord the following summer, 1820. He promised that, should he himself not be able to carry out the survey, an associate would come north to do it.[105] Grimes placed his furs in Peter Dobell's care and arranged to have them shipped to Joseph H. Gardner, his agent in Okhotsk, instructing Gardner to sell them "to the

[100]It appears that Grimes is referring to an espontoon.

[101]It is interesting that Grimes did not mention selling alcohol. It is probable that at that time the native inhabitants of the Bering Strait region were unacquainted with alcoholic beverages.

[102]Petropavlovsk, Kamchatka.

[103]A voyage to the Northwest Coast of North America.

[104]Grimes to Ebbets.

[105]Grimes (from Canton) to Dobell (Manila), March 11, 1820, Eliab Grimes Business Letter Book; Lazarev 1950:214–215.

best advantage" and to forward the proceeds to Meyer and Bruxner, agents in St. Petersburg, Russia, who would divide the credit equally between "Messrs Boardman & Pope of Boston and John Jacob Astor of New York."[106]

The *General San Martín* then headed to Hawaii, and there, on December 15, 1819, William J. Pigot bought her from her owners, William Heath Davis and Thomas Meek, for $10,000. As we have seen however, prior to the *General San Martín*'s arrival in the North, the owners had agreed to sell her to the King of Hawaii for 2500 piculs of sandalwood, payable on her return, but King Kamehameha died on May 8, 1819, and the agreement was not concluded. Pigot immediately sent her to Manila.[107]

[106]Grimes to Joseph H. Gardner (Okhotsk), September 21, 1819 and Grimes to Meyer and Bruxner (St. Petersburg), September 21, 1819, Eliab Grimes Business Letter Book.

[107]Porter 1932:281, Pierce 1990:399–400; Daws 1968:55; Grimes to Ebbets, September 21, 1819.

Chapter 2

The Voyages of the Pedler *and the* Blagonamerennyi *(1820)*

On the same day, December 15, 1819, Eliab Grimes wrote to Petr Rikord, answering a letter that Rikord had sent to Pigot (which Grimes himself probably carried to Hawaii). No doubt as a consequence of the agreement that Rikord and Grimes had reached in September, Rikord had written to Pigot asking about undertaking further "surveys and discoveries for and on Acct of Count Romanzoff[108]." Grimes replied to Rikord that it was necessary for him (Grimes) to "proceed to America for the Purpose of procuring a suitable Vessel of Cargo for this Ocean. . .," adding, with his eye firmly focused on the bottom line, that "it is very uncertain that I shall go to the North[,] as the amount of property that can be collected is so small it will not be worth going for while there is other business of more profit, but should I go that way I will give you all the information that I am capable of[,] should I have time & not interfere with my business."[109] As we shall see, however, Pigot did in fact agree to Rikord's request and did go north in 1820.

Shortly after replying to Rikord, Grimes took passage to Boston aboard Boardman and Pope's ship *Eagle*, with Thomas Meek in command.[110] Later, in Canton, Grimes wrote to Dobell in Manila, reaffirming his reluctance to return to Bering Strait. Grimes asked Dobell to send word to Rikord via one of his vessels, informing Rikord again that it would not be possible for him (Grimes) to carry out Count Rumiantsev's request for further explorations in that region because "it is not certain that I shall go to the North on Acct of the small Amt of property that can be collected."[111]

While in Canton, Grimes also received a letter via Astor's agent there, Nicholas Gouverneur Ogden.[112] The letter was from John Ebbets in New York, informing Grimes that Astor was in Europe and that it was unlikely

---

108Count Nikolai Petrovich Rumiantsev.

109Grimes to Rikord, December 15, 1819, Eliab Grimes Business Letter Book.

110Howay 1973:120–121; Malloy 1998:97; Grimes to Pigot, March 10, 1820, Eliab Grimes Business Letter Book.

111Grimes to Dobell, March 11, 1820, Eliab Grimes Business Letter Book. Grimes reached Boston and sailed again for the Pacific in command of the brig *Inore* which reached Hawaii, having been damaged by a storm, in May 1821, and, after repairs, was sold to the King of Hawaii. Grimes then took command of the Eagle and departed for the coast of California on a smuggling cruise (Howay 1973:147–148).

112Porter 1931:607.

that he (Ebbets) would "be able to send a Vessel out this season."[113] Astor, far-sighted as always, was reassessing his commitment to the Pacific trade. "I have understood," Grimes continued, "that Mr. Astor is not pleased with the result of the Voyage—We understand that Mr. Astor is getting rather indifferent about business[,] however he has probably gone to Europe to make future arrangements."[114]

But Grimes probably knew that another of Astor's vessels would fulfill his promise of a further survey in the North, because at that date the brig *Pedler*[115] (225 tons, with eight thirty-pound guns) was well underway from New York and about to reach Hawaii. Late in 1819 the 225-ton *Pedler* had set out from New York under the command of John Meek, Thomas Meek's brother, carrying a cargo of "gin, brown sugar, cloth and other goods."[116] She reached Honolulu on May 23, 1820, where, John Walters, the boatswain,[117] noted in his journal, "wee got our yellow legged lasses on board."[118] The *Pedler* also took aboard William J. Pigot, who was to serve as the ship's agent and supercargo and consequently would direct her movements during her trading cruise in the North.[119]

During June the *Pedler* cruised among the Hawaiian Islands and sold part of the cargo to "the vassal king of Kauai" for 191 piculs of sandalwood.[120] The *Pedler* then returned to Honolulu and John Meek took on fresh provisions and water for her northern cruise. The *Pedler* left the islands on June 23 "with a fine breeze to leave our copper coulard lasses," wrote John Walters.[121]

113Grimes to Pigot, March 10, 1820. In the autumn of 1820 Ebbets sailed from New York in the *William and John*, reaching Honolulu with a full cargo in April 1821 (Porter 1931:655).

114Grimes to Pigot. Among other reasons, Astor traveled to Europe for his own health and to seek psychiatric treatment for his eldest son, John Jacob Astor, Jr.

115The Pedler is listed as the *Pedlar* in some sources.

116Porter 1930:224–225; 1931:653.

117The boatswain, or bosun, was a ship's officer, or warrant officer, in charge of sails, rigging, anchors, cables, and all work on deck.

118John Walters, MS, journal, pp. 5–7. I am grateful to Dr. Mary Malloy for bringing this manuscript to my attention.

119Porter 1932: 282. A supercargo was a superintendent of a merchant ship's cargo. The supercargo was responsible for all commercial business during a voyage.

120Porter 1931:654; William J. Pigot and John Meek, contract with George Tamore, June 23, 1820, State Archives of Hawai'i, Honolulu.

121John Walters journal, p. 9.

The *Pedler* passed through the Aleutian Islands and entered the Bering Sea. On July 20 she reached Saint Lawrence Island ("Clarks Island") "at the entrance to the straits"[122] and, after having sailed nearly 3000 miles from Hawaii, "came to anchor in 10 fathoms[.] wee got the natives off to trade[.] they brout furs and sea horse teeth and wee gave them small quantity of tobaco and beads and so forth in return[.] while lying to anchor saw A ship[.] we got under way and spoke her[.] she was A Russian on discovery."[123]

Acting on Grimes' information about the region, Pigot had directed Captain Meek to anchor the *Pedler* at the northwestern tip of Saint Lawrence Island. This is where she lay when the Russian naval vessel *Otkrytie [Discovery]* came upon her. The *Otkrytie* was under the command of Captain-Lieutenant Mikhail Nikolaevich Vasil'ev, the leader of the northern section of a four-ship voyage of discovery. The *Otkrytie*, inbound from Petropavlovsk, was headed to Kotzebue Sound to rendezvous with the *Blagonamerennyi* [*Loyal*, or *Good Intent*], and from there they were to search for a northwest passage, across the top of North America, to the Atlantic. The *Otkrytie* overhauled the *Pedler* to ask whether the Americans had seen her partner.[124]

The Americans had not seen her, and the *Pedler* moved onward, probably to Saint Lawrence Bay on Grimes' advice. Walters continued, "we stood for the continent Asia and hove two off a vilage and a few of the natives came off but not willing to trade[.] we sent one man on shore to see if they wold trade[,] we keeping some off the natives on board till the man returned which was the next morning and they wold not trade with us."[125] It is puzzling that the natives would not trade with the *Pedler's* man; perhaps Chukchi traders had already collected all the furs.

---

[122]The straits" was a term loosely and variously used by nineteenth century American mariners to include the waters lying between the approximate latitudes of Saint Lawrence Island (63°N.) and Bering Strait (66°N.) (Bockstoce and Batchelder 1978:260).

[123]John Walters journal, p. 10.

[124]Lazarev 1950:383–384. Vasil'ev records the date as 13 July (Gregorian calendar).

[125]John Walters, journal, p. 10.

On July 25 the *Pedler* reached King Island. The fact that Pigot headed there before going to Kotzebue Sound suggests that, acting on Grimes' information, he may have been trying to intercept the flow of furs before they reached the Chukchi traders. "The natives came on board," wrote Walters, "and we trated for fur and ivory and giving tobaco and beads in return[.] The natives seem to bea friendly[.]

The Americans perceived the King Island Eskimos not to be hostile — contrary to Grimes' apparent assessment of their intentions the year before. Some of the King Islanders, the *Ukiuvaŋmiut*,[126] were, of course, on board the *Pedler*, where they were presumably outnumbered by the brig's crew of about thirty, and probably therefore behaved passively; on shore, however, with the numbers reversed, they might have acted very differently. In any case, Pigot must have felt comfortable enough in allowing one of them to have a firearm, about which the King Islanders were apparently ignorant. "we let the chief have a musket[.] they not noing the use of it[,] but we showed them by firing it off[.]"[127]

Walters then witnessed the first recorded encounter between an inhabitant of the Bering Strait region and a pig. "I see one of them come forward and we had some hages [hogs] under the boat which grunted[.] that frightened the fellow that he run aft in such a hurry that he fell his lenth on the deck as if the divil was after him[.]"[128]

Walters described the King Islanders: "broad faces and eyes resenbling the chinius [Chinese][.] it is hard to till the woman from the man by their dress[,] but I see some of them very handsom featurd[.] their clothing is of rain deer skin and cama links[129] that is made of sea lion guts and throtes neatly sewed together which is fine for standing water[.] their ornaments is ivory curiously carved which they do with stones."[130]

[126]Burch 1998b:33.

[127]Two years later, in 1822, the chief's son, Kunaginyn, asked Vasilii Stepanovich Khramchenko (who was in command of the Russian American Company's brig *Golovnin*) for gunpowder, presumably for this firearm. (Khramchenko MS:93).

[128]John Walters, journal, pp. 10–11.

[129]*Kamleika*, an Aleut term, often used by the Russians to denote rainwear made from sea mammal intestines.

[130]John Walters, journal, p. 11.

Walters may also have gone ashore on King Island. "they live in caves underground that will hold a number of them," Walters continued. "they have a small entrance to goin and keps a fier of blubber that smells disagreable but keeps them from the cold wether. . .[.] they are imployed in hunting and fishing for sea horse and whale[,] seal and so forth[.] all this done with spears and bows and arrows made of sea horse teeth[.] their boats is slightly formed and covered with sea horse hide when dried[.] their diet is of the sea horse[,] blubber oil and fish. they [have] no bread or any thing of the like amongst them[.] they seem to live happy in their way."[131]

The *Pedler* then continued on north, through Bering Strait and toward Kotzebue Sound. The Americans were unaware that the Otkrytie's partner-in-discovery, the *Blagonamerennyi*, was already in Kotzebue Sound. On July 22, 1820,[132] the *Blagonamerennyi*, about five days ahead of the *Otkrytie*, reached near Cape Espenberg, the southernmost of the two points of land[133] that enclose Kotzebue Sound.

Midshipman Nikolai Dmitrievich Shishmarev recorded their first encounter with the Eskimos of Kotzebue Sound.

> At 10:30 [P.M.] we saw a baidara [umiaq] coming toward us from Cape Espenberg. On its approach we saw 7 people in it, all paddling hard. . . We began to shout to them "Tavvakom," that is, tobacco, thinking that they were as fond of it as on [Saint] Lawrence Island. Though they answered us, we did not understand; but soon they set course directly for us, meanwhile having held a red fox [skin] on a pole. We immediately could understand that they wanted to trade furs with us. As soon as they came alongside the captain[134] immediately gave them a little

131John Walters, journal, p. 12.

132Nikolai Shishmarev listed his dates per the Julian ("Old Style") calendar, which in the nineteenth century was twelve days behind the Gregorian ("New Style") calendar. I have added twelve days to Shishmarev's dates to convert them to the Gregorian date; thus Shishmarev's July 10 is given here as July 22. Nikolai Shishmarev, MS, microfilm reel 15, item 101, Shur Collection, Alaska and Polar Regions Department, University of Alaska, Fairbanks. The original is in the Russian State Naval Archive (RGAVMF), Fond 203, opis' 1, delo 730[b].

133The northern point of land that encloses Kotzebue Sound is Cape Krusenstern.

134The captain of the *Blagonamerennyi* had been there before. Captain-Lieutenant Gleb Semenovich Shishmarev had served as senior officer under Otto von Kotzebue aboard the *Riurik* on the voyage of 1815 to 1818. I assume that he was a relative of Nikolai Shishmarev.

Illustration 7. Eskimos of Kotzebue Sound offering trade goods to the crew of HMS *Blossom*, 1826.
From James Wolfe, *Journal of a Voyage on Discovery in the Pacific and Beering's Straits.*
Credits: Western Americana Collection, Beinecke Rare Book and Manuscript Library, Yale University.

tobacco, and for this they gave one fox. However, we could barter nothing from them, because they are so seasoned in trade that they are not inferior to our bazaar merchants. . . . For example, they did not want to take knives, scissors, needles, mirrors, and other such things; and if someone looked at something, he examined it with great attention and the slightest rust or damage did not appeal to them and they gave it back. Their demands were for axes."[135]

The Eskimos then left the Russians.

"at 12:30 we again saw 4 baidaras a little bigger than the first coming toward us, which soon fearlessly came alongside. In them were 42 people in all, the same sort of traders as the first. At the top of their voices they beckon toward themselves and try to barter something, but they price their things so high that it was impossible to barter anything. Their demands were the same as those of the first, and in half an hour they all left the vessel. One must note that there was a woman in one baidara, a real fury; with disheveled black hair...she shouted ceaselessly with all her might."[136]

[135]Axes were not part of the Eskimo tool kit. It is probable that the Eskimos wanted to acquire axe heads to haft them horizontally—not vertically, as the blade of an axe would be fastened to its handle—thus creating adzes. See, for instance, Bockstoce 1977:72.

[136]Nikolai Shishmarev MS, F. 203, op. 1, d. 730[b], f.54v–55v.

Aleksei Petrovich Lazarev, a lieutenant aboard the *Blagonamerennyi*, also described meeting the Eskimos from Cape Espenberg and added some details about them, although he conflated the two encounters that Nikolai Shishmarev reported.

> We had an encounter with the American savages from the western settlement of Cape Espenberg. They came to us 48 strong in five baidaras [umiaqs] and wanted to barter their furs, but we did not take them and instead gave them gifts of tobacco and other trifles. The savages came directly alongside our sloop straightaway, but not one of them dared to come aboard no matter how much we tried to persuade them. They were dressed in ground squirrel or muskrat parkas, very neatly sewn, and almost all had perforations under the lower lip at the corners of the mouth in which was stuck a large sky blue bead set with bone or stones of various colors.[137] It seems that one can recognize their elders by this decoration because some of them had a bead of larger size and better set than the others. Near their ears and nose[,] down the whole length of the face were pricked various figures, and they are always ready to make a new hole any place in their face in order to pass through it a thread of worthless beads given to them.; they especially chose sky blue ones. We wanted to barter weapons from them, but they tried to sell foxes instead, for each of which they requested either an ax or a large knife, but as we did not need this trade item of theirs to make up our collection of curios, we gave them gifts of tobacco alone, to which they scarcely paid attention. For each trifle they asked a very high price and tried to substitute another, poorer item for an item already sold, for example a dog's tail for a marten, etc."[138]

[137]Labrets, piercing the lower lips, were often worn by Iñupiaq males. Large blue beads, which presumably were made in China (Miller 1994:18–24), were particularly valued and, cut in half, were fixed to the labrets (Bockstoce 1977:87–90). The size and quantity of beads worn by the Eskimos were indicators, of wealth.

[138]Lazarev 1950:199–200. Lazarev gives the date as July 21 (New Style).

On August 29, 1826 the crew of HMS Blossom witnessed similar trickery on the Choris Peninsula. Frederick William Beechey described trading for fish with the Eskimos: "On several occasions, however, they tried to impose upon us with fish-skins, ingeniously put together to represent a whole fish, though entirely deprived of their original contents: but this artifice succeeded only once: the natives, when detected in other attempts, laughed heartily, and treated the affair as a fair practical joke" (Beechey 1831: I, 285; Bockstoce 1977:109–110).

Shishmarev's and Lazarev's reports reveal several things about the native inhabitants of Cape Espenberg. The Eskimos apparently had adequate supplies of tobacco, suggesting that they had already sold some of their furs to native traders that summer and had received tobacco in return. Iron tools and weapons were valued commodities. Furthermore the natives were masterful traders, well acquainted with deceitful maneuvers. The fact that they approached the Russian ship without apparent hesitation suggests that they had by then become somewhat accustomed to the sight of foreign vessels, and the fact that they approached with a large number of persons suggests that they were more comfortable in force when encountering foreigners.

The *Blagonamerennyi* then continued into Kotzebue Sound and anchored at Chamisso Island. On July 25, while awaiting the *Otkrytie's* arrival, Captain Shishmarev decided to send an expedition comprising a longboat and a three-hatch Aleutian kayak to explore Eschscholtz Bay. Captain Shishmarev no doubt remembered the antagonistic reception the *Riurik's* men had received in 1816 on the north coast of the Seward Peninsula, so he outfitted the longboat with, among other things, fifteen armed sailors and four falconets.[139]

And in the same frame of mind, when Lieutenant Aleksei Lazarev went ashore near Elephant Point, seeing a large number of Eskimos encamped there, he wrote: "I was in high Aleut boots and was the first to get out to wade, having small pocket pistols loaded with bullets up my sleeves. The inhabitants immediately met me, but with great distrustfulness, especially the elder, who maintained an average of about a hundred paces between me and their throng. The savages tried by all means not to come close to me, though I showed them that I had nothing in my hands, to which the elder replied with the same sign."

To judge from other encounters, it is probable that this elder, like Lazarev, also had weapons concealed in his sleeves. Nevertheless, when

[139] Light cannons, usually on swivels.

Lazarev "showed them some tobacco and other things, all distrustfulness on their side apparently disappeared, the elder beckoned the others, and they all ran directly up to me." The Eskimos then "sat on the ground in a semi-circle, and," Lazarev continued, "sat me before them in the middle and began to greet me, blowing their nose in their hand and then smearing it on the face, to which I responded in the same manner."[140]

The Russians must have been surprised to find so many natives at the place where Kotzebue had not reported seeing anyone.[141] In fact Kotzebue had arrived there in the latter part of August, 1816—after the Buckland River Eskimos (the *Kaŋiġmiut*) had dispersed following the conclusion of their annual congregation to hunt belukha whales—whereas the *Blagonamerennyi's* men had reached there more than three weeks earlier, probably just as the hunt was completed.[142]

Despite the friendly start to their encounter, the Eskimos soon became aggressive, and, while Lazarev and a few other Russians climbed the bluff behind the encampment, the Eskimos gathered around them and began to cut the gold buttons from his uniform. In response Lazarev vigorously shoved one of the men away, adding, "one should by no means allow them impudence or boldness."[143] On their way back to the longboat the Russians passed through the Eskimo encampment again and found that an armed native stood in front of each tent and each umiaq (which was ready for immediate launching). "Here the inhabitants again followed us and did not go away," he added, "very much desiring and even insistently demanding that we trade with them."

After the Russians had eaten a meal at the longboat, Captain Shishmarev allowed the crew to trade with the Eskimos, and the natives' hard-headed approach to bartering was reaffirmed to the Russians. "But no one of us could succeed in this trade," Lazarev wrote, "because the

---

[140]Lazarev 1950:201–202.

[141]Kotzebue 1821b:218–222.

[142]For details of the *Kaŋiġmiut* belukha hunt see, for instance, Burch 1998a:273–277.

[143]Lazarev 1950:202.

[Eskimos][144] charged much too high a price for each thing requested [,] an axe or large knife, which we did not have with us."[145]

The Russians then decided to return to the *Blagonamerennyi,* but as soon as they had launched the longboat, an onshore wind put up such a steep sea that it not only prevented them from tacking offshore, but also soaked them all, including their weapons. They had no choice but to return to shore to dry out and await a change in the weather. Lazarev described their situation: "One must admit that at this time our situation was very unpleasant. Our guns, musketoons,[146] pistols, and even falconets had become completely drenched, so that it was necessary to unload, swab, and clean them. There remained only a few lances and cutlasses for our defense. [The Eskimos], as we later saw, each had several knives: one up the left sleeve, another down the right boot, and a third, about half an arshin[147] long, along the back between the shoulder blades. . . ."[148]

The Russians were now in a very dangerous situation. Forced ashore and unable to reach the safety of their ship, their firearms inoperative, they were outnumbered roughly ten-to-one by a group of heavily armed, aggressive Eskimos. Unfortunately for the men from the *Blagonamerennyi,* in the early nineteenth century it was a fact of life that the Eskimo nations of northwestern Alaska were constantly alert to the possibility of attack from other nations; consequently *all* strangers were considered to be, *sui generis,* dangerous enemies unless they could prove otherwise.

The ethnohistorian Ernest S. Burch, Jr. has concisely summarized the Eskimo attitude toward strangers. "The evidence from both oral and written sources confirms that the Iñupiat were not the happy, peaceful hunter-gatherers of anthropological perspective. Instead they were fiercely inde-

[144]Lazarev uses the term Americans. To avoid confusion I have inserted Eskimos throughout. In 1826 Frederick William Beechey was the first person to positively identify the natives of northwestern Alaska as Eskimos (Bockstoce 1977:16).

[145]Lazarev 1950:204.

[146]Musketoon: A short, large-bore musket.

[147]A Russian linear measure. An arshin is equal to 28 inches (approximately 71 cm).

[148]Lazarev 1950:206.

pendent peoples who conducted external affairs in a very aggressive manner. Armed conflict, and the threat of armed conflict, were basic facts of life."[149] As we have already noted, in encounters when explorers outnumbered the natives, the Eskimos were usually docile, but when the Eskimos found themselves in superior numbers to the visitors, they rapidly pressed their advantage, becoming extremely belligerent and domineering.[150]

Lazarev then tried to intimidate the Eskimos by firing the Russians' only operative gun, but his bluff failed. "Seeing our disproportion to them both in numbers and in strength," Lazarev went on, "it came into my head to inspire fear in them in advance. For this I pulled out of a box my own gun, the only one that had remained dry, and, having fired at a sea gull flying by, killed it. The inhabitants at first were frightened by this, and all shrieked from fright, but when they saw that the whole thing had ended with the death of one bird, they began to laugh loudly and one of them, having grabbed a stone, also killed a sea gull flying by, and rather high, after which he explained to us that the effect of both implements was the same. His other comrades then demonstrated their skill in throwing stones by hand, hitting the mark at about fifty paces. . . ."[151]

Forced to spend the night ashore, the Russians set up a tent and posted sentries. Lazarev continued his report.

> It was already around 10 o'clock in the evening and we, desiring to set ourselves at ease, tried with all our might to convince the inhabitants to leave us. For a long time they did not understand us, or perhaps they did not want to obey. Seeing that they continued to surround the tent, one of the Aleuts with us who knew a few words of the Agalakhmut[152] language, through it and pantomime made them understand our wishes. After that he ran very quickly and began to make a line in the earth around the tent right by the watchmen, explaining that during the

149Burch 1998b:49.

150Burch 1998b:46–47.

151Lazarev 1950:206–207.

152Lazarev is probably referring to the Aglurmiut, an Eskimo society that inhabited the northeastern part of the Alaska Peninsula (VanStone 1984:225, 241).

night no one should cross it. Some of the inhabitants still stood near us and watched this work, but when the line was close to completing the circle they all threw themselves headlong outside it as if fearing some sorcery. Having stood awhile near the line, they made a line of their own about five paces from ours and indicated to the watchmen through pantomime that they should not cross it. After this they made faces and laughed for another half hour and finally dispersed to the settlement and did not come all night. Seeing the savages dispersing, we lay down to sleep and spent the night rather peacefully, but in great caution, inspecting the watchmen very frequently and conducting the shift changes ourselves, giving them necessary instructions. At midnight all the wet guns were in order and in readiness in case of attack, for which, however, we had not given the slightest grounds, treating the inhabitants very kindly and having given them various things.

At 3 am, when it was just getting light, the inhabitants began little by little to gather. . .but the watchmen did not allow them to come farther. This apparently insulted the [Eskimos], and they told our sailors that they should not come up on them, either, laughed at them, and some even began to break through, waving and threatening with their large knives. The watchmen alerted us of this with their shout. All those sleeping in the tent were awakened by this noise and we feared bad consequences. I went out first and began to greet the inhabitants and soon after me appeared the captain, who...ordered our watchmen to come to the tent, having indicated to the savages that they too could come there. This restored calm and barter began, just as unprofitable for us as on the day before because for every little thing they requested from us either an axe or a knife. The captain wanted to barter a [kayak] and the deal had already been made when suddenly the axe offered for it did not appeal to the seller because it bore several spots of rust.

During this trade I walked about between our people and the [Eskimos] watching that nothing unpleasant should happen between them, which in fact happened and could have led to very bad consequences if I had not averted them with presents. The barter, as I have already noted, took place at the persistent insistence of the inhabitants and we were forced, whether we wanted to or not, to buy what they offered us, even what was entirely unnecessary for us. It happened that one sailor, having bought one of two ermines that were tied together, began to cut away one with a knife and accidentally cut the hand of the seller, who was still holding both furs. Grumbling and noise immediately began and if I had not given a gift to their wounded man, all his comrades could have been outraged and then it would have been difficult for us, 15 men, to settle with 200 who had three knives apiece and were masterful users of slings etc.

Soon after this I stopped in at our tent and saw in it a savage [Eskimo], a robust man, who was examining a pistol I had left on the table. It was loaded, at half-cock, and the [Eskimo] was touching it without any caution and was looking directly into the muzzle. Fearing the consequences that could arise from this, I approached him, took the pistol and, pointing the muzzle away from him, tried to explain by signs that the pistol could fire and kill him. The savage probably understood me differently, i.e., that I would kill him for touching the pistol; in an instant he flew into a rage and with flashing eyes struck me in the left side near the stomach with his spear. Fortunately it only penetrated the warm overcoat, waistcoat, and trousers I was wearing and stopped after scratching the skin. I had not yet had time to think when he seized his long knife from behind his back and threatened me, while the spear remained with its shaft on the floor and the stone [point] in me.

Seeing the brutality of the savage and his eyes, so to speak, flashing with malice, and fearing to be the reason for further quarrels between us and the [Eskimos] and through that, of course, guilty of the death of many, I was silent, waving my hand and indicating that I was not afraid of threats. Fortunately, at the same time one of the sailors,

Sal'nikov, came into the tent, and soon another as well. The [Eskimo], having seen them, with a look of extreme cold-bloodedness, put the knife back in its sheath, extracted his spear, and very quietly left the tent."[153]

Not long thereafter things cooled off somewhat between the Russians and the Eskimos, and, "at the invitation of the elder," Lazarev went on, "the captain and I crawled into his [tent] where sat two...women. Its interior was

[153]Lazarev 1950:207–209. I have added paragraph indentations.

Midshipman Karl Karlovich Gillesem of the *Blagonamerennyi* also wrote an account of this encounter between the Eskimos and the Russians (Gillesem 1849, Vol. 55, No. 10; Ray 1983:25–54; Ray and Josephson 1971). Curiously enough, he mentions that a few of the Eskimos there possessed muskets and that they wanted to trade for gunpowder and lead. He also describes an incident wherein Lazarev's pistol was accidentally discharged into an Eskimo's face. Gillesem furthermore states that, as the Russians rowed toward their ship in their longboat, the Eskimos fired their guns at them and the Russians returned the fire with their falconet (Ray 1992:68–69). Neither Lazarev nor Nikolai Shishmarev mentioned these details.

Regarding the possibility that the *Kaŋiġmiut* already possessed firearms, Ernest S. Burch, Jr. (2003:412–413) has pointed out that the Eskimos of the same region were ignorant of firearms four years earlier (1816), when Kotzebue visited the area. And in 1826 and 1827, when the Beechey expedition was there, no Eskimos were reported to have firearms (Bockstoce 1977:104-132). Kotzebue (1821b, I:205) described a tense encounter with the Eskimos at Shishmaref Inlet in 1816, "I myself threatened them with my gun, pointing it sometimes at one, and sometimes at another; but this had no effect on them; they laughed heartily, and only waited for more troops to attempt a serious attack upon us. As our firearms, *with which they were wholly unacquainted* [emphasis added], gave us superiority, and protected us from every danger, we patiently bore all their provocations...." Later, near the mouth of the Nugnugaluktuk River in Goodhope Bay, he wrote, "I observed a snipe, and wishing to know if my companions [the Eskimos] were acquainted with fire-arms...I was induced to shoot it. The sound occasioned the greatest fright, they looked at each other, not knowing whether to stay or fly. . . The dead snipe...inspired...the greatest respect for the [gun], and they could not get over their astonishment...." (Kotzebue 1821b, I:229).

As we have seen from Eliab Grimes' report to John Ebbets about the 1819 cruise, the only firearms that were reported to have been traded from the *General San Martín* were a pair of old pistols, *somewhere* in the Bering Strait region.

Gillesem's account of his voyage in the Pacific seems to be reliable in many other details—and in some cases can be verified by the other reports—but his mention of the Eskimos possessing firearms in Kotzebue Sound cannot be confirmed. Gillesem's narrative was published 27 years after the event (Ray 1983:63). It seems to me that Gillesem may have written his account some years after the voyage took place and, in the passage of time, had confused some of the details. For example, in his description of events in 1820 he mentions meeting American trading brigs three times (in Kotzebue Sound, in Novo-Arkhangel'sk, and in Hawaii) and apparently recalled having met two separate vessels. But in fact, all three encounters were with the *Pedler* (which he does not identify by name). In the Kotzebue Sound and Hawaiian encounters he identifies the brig's captain as Pigot (who was actually the *Pedler's* supercargo), but in the Novo-Arkhangel'sk encounter the brig's captain is correctly identified as Meek.

My earlier references to Eskimos possessing firearms in the incident at Elephant Point in 1820 (Bockstoce 1977:6-7; 1986:180) were based on Gillesem's account (Ray 1975, Ray and Josephson 1971).

Nevertheless, firearms may already have been working their way toward the Bering Strait region. Kotzebue noticed a musket (which neither Choris, the expedition's artist, nor Chamisso, the expedition's naturalist, mentioned) among the natives on the west side of Bering Strait, near East Cape (Mys Dezhneva), and he assumed that the natives had acquired it from Russian traders—presumably via one of the trading centers in northeastern Asia (Kotzebue 1821a:156; 1821b:245). On the other hand, Frederick Lütké, who surveyed the eastern shore of the Chukchi Peninsula in 1828, stated that the Chukchi did not have firearms and pointed out that it was forbidden to sell these weapons to them at the trade fairs (Lütké 1835:II, 266–267).

On the assumption that it is unlikely that any trading vessels had preceded Kotzebue's ship to Bering Strait, the only other (and equally unlikely) sources for the musket could have been from previous discovery expeditions.

filled with fish, fat, guts, and every sort of filth. The master showed us his wealth, consisting of knives, cutlasses, and other iron things of very clean finish which, he explained, he had received from the Hudson's Bay Company.[154]

"The weapons of this people are bows and arrows which they keep in sewn skin quivers and which have sharp worked flints on the ends. Their lances are also of plain wood and were often, it seems, of driftwood with worked flint on the end. As food they use, we saw, walrus, seal, and whale meat and fat, small fish which they roast simply, throwing them on the coals, and birds, roasted in the same manner. Near each hut there were no fewer than four dogs. Of furs they have red fox, beaver, arctic fox, and bear skins."[155]

"On this stretch of shore grows [*Ledum*],"[156] Lazarev added, "which the inhabitants mix with tobacco in order to get intoxicated more quickly. The local [Eskimos] are terribly fond of smoking-tobacco. Having filled a wooden pipe with it and having mixed it with [*Ledum*] (and when there is none, they are satisfied with the latter herb alone), the [Eskimos] when smoking draw in all the smoke and hold it for at least five minutes, until they become intoxicated and completely lose consciousness. In this condition they begin retching and it goes on for more than a quarter of an hour until they regain consciousness. When they stand up after this, judging from their faces one can suppose that they have come from great intoxication. We saw this more than once among the [Eskimos] in the settlement in Eschscholtz Bay."[157]

The Russians returned to their ship, and a few days later, to their joy, the *Otkrytie*, hove into sight. The *Otkrytie*, having visited Petropavlovsk,

---

[154]Lazarev's reference to the Hudson's Bay Company seems to be his misunderstanding of his informants' reports. There is no evidence that Hudson's Bay Company trade goods had reached the Bering Strait region by that date. At that time the closest abundant source of metals was from the Russian trading centers in northeastern Asia.

[155]Lazarev 1950:210–211.

[156]Lazarev identifies it as *bagul'nik*, which is *Ledum* (sp.), a small circumpolar shrub which is occasionally used as a substitute for tea and is variously called "Hudson Bay tea" or "Labrador tea." *Ledum palustre*, which is abundant in the Kotzebue Sound region, contains ledol "a poisonous substance causing cramps and paralysis" (Hultén 1968:717).

[157]Lazarev 1950:211.

was carrying "news and letters from our friends and relatives," wrote Lazarev.[158] Captain-lieutenant Mikhail Nikolaevich Vasil'ev and the officers of the *Otkrytie* then came aboard the *Blagonamerennyi* to dine, when, to the surprise of the Russians, a third ship appeared. She was, of course, the *Pedler*, and John Walters, a man of few words, noted their arrival: "anchored in scots pru [Kotzebue] sound. . .found two Russian ships on discovery."[159]

Lazarev also described the *Pedler's* arrival. "In the second hour[160] there arrived from sea a brig under the flag of the United American States and, having anchored between our sloops,[161] it saluted with seven shots, to which the Otkrytie replied with five per the regulations of Emperor Petr I.

"In the seventh hour of the evening Clark, former supercargo with our consul Dobrel[162] in Manila, came to our sloop from the American brig. He declared to us that the name of his brig was *Pedler*, cargo owner Pigot, captain John Meek, that there were 30 men aboard, and that they had come here to barter furs from the inhabitants in exchange for leather, sabers, guns, powder, etc. . ." "One must admit," Lazarev continued with a certain amount of admiration, "that the enlightened Americans are expeditious in trade; they scarcely hear of some new discovery before they appear there with trade goods. Captain Vasil'ev, passing by St. Lawrence Island on the way to Kotzebue Sound, saw the aforementioned brig and questioned it. Clark brought us a few pineapples as a gift, a great rarity among the polar ice and snow."[163]

---

[158]Lazarev 1950:213.

[159]John Walters, journal, p. 13.

Walters' journal and the Russian reports of the meeting of the three ships in Kotzebue Sound in 1820 do not agree precisely as to the date, when adjusted for the Julian-Gregorian difference of twelve days. These discrepancies, I assume, arose from the fact that Walters' account was apparently written later, from notes, and the Russian accounts were kept in both nautical time (wherein the new day was reckoned to start at noon) and civil time (wherein the new day began at midnight). Furthermore, the Russians had sailed to Bering Strait eastward, via the Cape of Good Hope, whereas the *Pedler* had sailed from New York westward, via Cape Horn, thus adding the uncertainly of the calculation of the date change near what was later to become the International Date Line.

[160]Lazarev was recording his journal in nautical time. The second hour is between 1 and 2 pm.

[161]The ships were rated as sloops.

[162]Peter Dobell. As we have seen, Dobell was not, in fact, the Russian consul in Manila because his credentials had been rejected by the Spanish government. Clark had been his agent in Petropavlovsk while Dobell was in St. Petersburg (Porter 1932:272).

[163]Lazarev 1950:214.

Lazarev then reviewed his understanding of why the *Pedler* had appeared in Kotzebue Sound. "When the *Otkrytie* was in Kamchatka this summer, the commander of Kamchatka, Rikord, told Captain Vasil'ev that the year before [1819] the American [Grimes],[164] who was aboard a vessel also belonging to Pigot,[165] allegedly went, on the commission of Count Nikolai Petrovich Rumiantsev, to verify the discoveries made in the north by Kotzebue.[166] On his return to Petropavlovsk port in the fall, [Grimes] told the commander of Kamchatka that on his trip beyond Bering Strait he stopped at Shishmarev Bay, whence he explored the whole area right up to Kotzebue Sound and the sound itself and went in a longboat near the whole coast, measuring the depth with a pole. According to him, these places are very incorrectly placed on the chart and are even not at all as they should be. Finally, with regard to the strait in Goodhope Bay, so named by Kotzebue, he expected from the name that this strait would lead to the north, as Kotzebue maintained. 'From these stories,' said Captain Rikord, 'it is apparent that [Grimes] is a man who had taken on something that is not in his line of work.'"

Lazarev, apparently overlooking the fact that a longboat could work very close to shore in shallow water, then interjected: "In fact, can one measure depth in a sound with a pole when in some places it goes to 15 sazhens?"[167]

"[Grimes] said also that next year, i.e., in 1820, if not he then another vessel would come for further explorations and the brig we met justified those words."[168]

"Curiosity compelled Captain Shishmarev to go aboard the American brig, having invited me with him, to look at the chart made by [Grimes], the more so as he himself [Captain Shishmarev] had been a participant in placing the coast and sound on Kotzebue's chart. On arriving aboard the brig we

164Lazarev identifies the man's name as "Grey." He is referring to Eliab Grimes.

165This was the General San Martín. In fact, as we have seen, her nominal owners were William Heath Davis and Thomas Meek. Eliab Grimes was both her captain and supercargo. Pigot bought the vessel after her return to Hawaii.

166As noted earlier, it seems clear that Rumiantsev had, in fact, encouraged a subsequent reconnaissance.

167A sazhen is a Russian linear measure equaling seven feet (approximately 2.134 m).

168Lazarev 1950:214–215.

saw that the aforesaid chart was nothing other than one crudely copied from Kotzebue's chart, on very thin transparent paper, and it was apparent that the Americans had not yet managed to transfer it to good paper. On it some insignificant changes were made with regard to capes and mountains, and in place of a strait in Goodhope Bay there was a lake."[169]

Although Lazarev suspected that Grimes had used his voyage more for a commercial reconnaissance than for a geographical survey on behalf of Count Rumiantsev (the Americans had, after all, borne the cost of the voyage themselves), the "strait" that appears in Goodhope Bay on Kotzebue's chart is, in fact, a saltwater lagoon, where the Nugnugaluktuk River debouches.

"Showing us this chart," Lazarev continued, "the Americans tried with all their might to convince us of its correctness, confirming [Grimes'] story that he allegedly measured all the places near shore with a pole and although he went along the coast he did not see a strait. When Shishmarev told them that he himself was in it and spent the night there, they immediately changed the subject and began to talk about the savages, asking us where we had seen them.

"Captain Rikord had given [Grimes] a sailor as an interpreter and that man was now aboard the *Otkrytie*. He said that the Americans did stop near Shishmarev Bay, but went no farther and though they went in a longboat, it was not for long enough to cover the whole distance from that bay to Kotzebue Sound. I do not think the merchant would have thought of covering this distance, nearly 200 versts,[170] in a longboat when one could sail aboard a vessel, and without any profit besides. Therefore, one can justly agree with Rikord's opinion that the Americans' goal was not discovery, but trade with the inhabitants for which they solicited a mission from Count Rumiantsev in order not to be hindered by that captain [Rikord] or our expedition. In addition, the

169Lazarev 1950:215.

170Approximately 132 statute miles. A verst is a Russian unit of linear measurement equal to 0.66 statute miles (1.07 km).

merchant-American really will not venture great expenditures without seeing personal profit."[171]

As we have seen, it is probable that it was *Rikord* who solicited Grimes' assistance, not the reverse. Lazarev may also have misunderstood the interpreter's account of where the *General San Martín* had gone while north of Bering Strait: The *General San Martín* did in fact reach the inner waters of Kotzebue Sound, and some reconnaissance was carried out with the ship's boat. Lazarev was also partly confused about the genesis of Grimes' voyage aboard the *General San Martín*. It is true that American traders were always alert for new trading opportunities throughout the Pacific, and Grimes was simultaneously aided in his commercial reconnaissance by Rikord (who had been encouraged by Rumiantsev) as a way of gaining geographical information for the Russians.

The following day the *Otkrytie* and *Blagonamerennyi* departed for explorations on the northwest coast of arctic Alaska, leaving the *Pedler* in Kotzebue Sound. Nevertheless, the Russians had cautioned the crew of the *Pedler* about being on their guard when dealing with the Eskimos in Eschscholtz Bay.[172]

"We advised [Pigot] to go to the smaller part of the sound as close as possible to the northeastern shores," Gillesem wrote, "but not to go on land, and to permit the Indians on the brig only after taking all precautions because these people were crafty and unreliable. As proof we related our adventures with them. . . ."[173]

The same day that the Russians departed, John Walters reported, "we sent our pinice[,][174] the chief officer[,] and 7 men to look for the natives to trade but being gon longer than was expected made us oneasy for fear of som accident. . .the boat returned with but litel sucksess[.] the same day we sailed down the straits."[175] The *Pedler* then headed for Kamchatka.

171Lazarev 1950:215–216.

172Gillesem 1849, Vol. 55, No. 10.

173Ray 1983:38.

174Pinnace: a small craft, or tender.

175John Walters, journal, pp. 13–14.

The *Pedler's* lack of success in trading with the Eskimos there suggests that the Eskimos, having heard the cannon fire from the ships' salutes, and seeing now *three* ships at anchor, perhaps dispersed or hid, believing that the foreigners might be returning in force with superior numbers and firepower. On the other hand, Ernest S. Burch, Jr. offers a different explanation. Burch writes: "It is equally likely that the Eskimos had headed inland to hunt caribou, which they would have done about this time [of year]. They weren't yet so addicted to trade that they would forego proper winter clothing to get it."[176]

It is interesting that the *Pedler's* voyage to Bering Strait was concluded much more quickly than the *General San Martín's* had been. If Grimes' and Walters' reports of their trading cruises included all the trading stops that each ship undertook, then it is clear that the *Pedler* touched only at those places where the *General San Martín* had traded successfully: Saint Lawrence Island, Saint Lawrence Bay, King Island, and Kotzebue Sound. The *Pedler's* trading cruise within the Bering Strait region only occupied eleven days; whereas the *General San Martín's* had taken forty-eight days. Thus, it appears that Pigot did in fact go north aboard the *Pedler* to confirm the conclusions that Grimes had drawn the year before. And the fact that the *Pedler* seems only to have acquired furs at Saint Lawrence Island and King Island, if true, would almost certainly have confirmed to the American traders that the effort and expense of a voyage to Bering Strait were not worth the reward.

On August 29 the *Pedler* anchored in Petropavlovsk's harbor, where they "made some trade with the govener [Rikord][.] He is a fine man," wrote Walters, "and speeks good English. . .We fired a salute on the Empirers birth day of 21 guns[.] The next day was visited by the govener and his lady which is a nice woman[.]"[177]

William Pigot told Rikord about the details of the *Pedler's* cruise in the

---

176Ernest S. Burch, Jr., personal communication, received April 15, 2004.

177John Walters, journal, pp. 14–15. Lyudmila Rikorda was apparently liked and respected by all who knew her.

Bering Strait region, about their encounters with the Otkrytie and Blagonamerennyi,[178] and, no doubt, about their relative lack of success in trading for furs. In return Rikord gave Pigot a letter of introduction to Matvei Ivanovich Murav'ev, the newly arrived chief manager of the Russian-American colonies[179] in Novo-Arkhangel'sk, the *Pedler*'s next port of call.

Continuing her cruise, the *Pedler* sailed from Petropavlovsk and endured a punishing eighteen-day (and nearly three thousand-mile) crossing of the North Pacific. When she reached Novo-Arkhangel'sk her hull was damaged, her sails were torn, and both boats, among other things, were broken up. It took the crew a month to repair the damage and build a new boat.[180] Before sailing for Hawaii, Pigot traded with Murav'ev for some of the *Pedler*'s cargo and took 2,620 fur seal skins in return for the trade goods.[181]

[178]Lazarev 1950:389–390; Rikord to Naval Ministry, 10 November 1820, Tsentralnyi Gosudarstvennyi Arkhiv Voennomorskogo Flota (RGAVMF) [Russian State Naval Archive], F. 166. d. 660, ch. II, ll. 269–270.

[179]Murav'ev to Main Office, No. 8, 18 January 1821, Records of the Russian-American Company, Correspondence of the Governors General, Communications sent, Vol. 2, [folios 130–133 verso], in: Fur Seal Arbitration, Vol. VIII, 1895:388.

[180]Murav'ev to Main Office.

[181]John Walters, journal, p. 15; Pierce 1990:368–371; Khlebnikov 1976:58.

Chapter 3

Aftermath

Shortly after the *Pedler's* departure for Russian America, startling news reached Petr Rikord in Petropavlovsk. A letter arrived from Count Mikhail Speranskii, the recently appointed Governor-General of Siberia. Although Siberia was "notorious for bad administration,"[182] Speranskii was an honest and diligent civil servant, and he was an energetic reformer who was greatly in favor of promoting Russian trade in the North Pacific. "These considerations," Marc Raeff wrote, "perhaps explain Speransky's [sic] favorable view of the Russo-American Company, whose monopolistic practices and plans were otherwise uncongenial to him." Nevertheless Speranskii was simultaneously "distrustful of American enterprise, in particular that of whalers and traders in the North Pacific, whose better commercial and organizational talents might provide 'unfair' competition for the Russians."[183]

Speranskii informed Rikord that, by imperial order, confirmed on March 31, 1820, the entire region was hereby closed to foreigners, and trade with foreigners was forbidden. Rikord was to annul the whaling agreement, which, as we have seen, he had entered with Pigot, Davis, Meek, and Ebbets. Foreigners were now forbidden to settle in Kamchatka and Okhotsk, and their ships were not allowed to visit the ports of Eastern Siberia. Furthermore, foreigners who were living in Kamchatka and Okhotsk were to be assisted in selling their houses and leaving. Moreover, Peter Dobell should cease sending his ships from Manila and henceforth should use Russian ships to send only cargoes of vital supplies. Thus, in response to the whaling initiative that Rikord had authorized in 1819, the objections of the Russian American Company (claiming infringement on its monopoly) had been fully upheld, despite the obvious hardship these restrictions would cause to the populace.[184]

This imperial order later reached Russian America. In a letter of January 21, 1821,[185] Murav'ev reported to the Russian American Company's

[182]Armstrong 1994:133.
[183]Raeff 1956:43.
[184]Vagin 1872:80—87.
[185]"Old style" (Julian calendar) date.

headquarters in St. Petersburg about the *Pedler's* visit to Novo-Arkhangel'sk. While Murav'ev no doubt welcomed the chance to acquire some supplies from the *Pedler*, he clearly was sensitive to the Company's position about maintaining its monopoly and about the stated undesirability of foreign trading vessels operating in the waters it claimed. Consequently, Murav'ev emphasized that the *Pedler's* arrival was the result of *force majeure,* and described the extent of the damage she had suffered.

Murav'ev explained that although Meek was the captain, "Pigott [sic] was the supercargo or owner; for the cargo was under his control, and he directed the movements of the ship. . . ."

> He brought with him a letter of recommendation from M. Ricord to me....I could not refuse him permission to anchor in the roadstead here and to repair his ship. . . . If I had refused to allow him to do this, I should have been violating the usage of friendly nations. I took care, however, to place rafts near his ship, and I informed him that if he violated the rights of the Colony in any way, or had any communications whatever with the Indians. . . . he would be at once arrested, and his ship and her cargo confiscated. Of course this annoyed him, and he told me so. I replied that I was justified in being suspicious of the open enemies of the Company. There were at that time two men-of-war on the roadstead,[186] and this fact afforded me frequent opportunities of meeting Pigott, for he was acquainted with the officers of both of them. They had met beyond Behring [sic] Strait in Kotzebue Sound, and had been anchored there together. He said in a hesitating way that he had been trading there, and complained that he had been unsuccessful; but are his statements to be believed?[187]
>
> He had a quantity of guns and ammunition with him, and sold some guns to the officers of the men-of-war. I asked him whether he had sold any guns in the north, and he answered that he had not; but are we to believe him?[188]

[186]The *Otkrytie* and *Blagonamerennyi.*

[187]As we have seen, Pigot sold a gun to a native at King Island.

[188]Murav'ev to Board of Management, January 21, 1821, in: Fur Seal Arbitration, Vol. VIII, 1895:388. Murav'ev was justifiably suspicious about the *Pedler*: In 1815, at Novo-Arkhangel'sk, the Russians had seized her briefly for trading gunpowder to the Indians (Pierce 1976:235, 241; Porter 1930:229; Malloy 1998:149).

The following year, to make matters worse for the inhabitants in eastern Asia and Russian America, Russia's isolationist policy of 1820 was strengthened by an imperial *ukaz*[189] of September 4, 1821,[190] "prohibiting foreign merchant ships from trading in the Russian colonies in the North Pacific." Thus, all whaling, fishing, and trading activities were forbidden to foreigners in waters that ran from Bering Strait, southward, to 51° N on the American coast and to 45°50′N on the Asian coast. Furthermore, no foreign vessel could approach the coast closer than 100 Italian miles.[191] That is, the Northwest Coast of America, from Queen Charlotte Sound northward, as well as the northeastern coast of Asia, most of the Kurile Islands, and the entire Sea of Okhotsk were closed to foreign men and ships.[192] By decree the Tsar had embargoed much of the northern North Pacific and adjacent waters as far north as the Arctic Ocean.

On September 13, 1821, a second imperial *ukaz* granted the Russian American Company a renewal of its charter and a monopoly over all activities within its territories for another twenty years.[193] This edict was underscored, specifically by the Minister of Foreign Affairs, warning American merchants (some of whom had been involved with gun running and rum running to the Northwest Coast Indians) not to trade with the natives there. Ships of the Imperial Navy would now be patrolling those coasts, and any vessel sailing from port after March 1, 1822, would be liable under these regulations for the confiscation of the vessel and her cargo.[194]

The Tsar's orders of 1820 and 1821—however short-sighted and unenforceable they may have been—had both defensive and offensive purposes. On the one hand they were aimed at American traders who ignored the Russian American Company's claimed monopoly on the Asian and American coasts, but they were also intended to block the advances of the Hudson's

[189]A decree, edict, or order from the Tsar.

[190]"Old style" (Julian calendar) date.

[191]115 statute miles. An Italian mile was equal to a nautical mile (one degree of latitude), or 1.15 statute miles.

[192]Dmytryshyn et al. 1989:339—352.

[193]Dmytryshyn et al. 1989: 353—366.

[194]Dmytryshyn et al. 1989:367—369; Gibson 1991:107.

Bay Company, whose traders were then approaching the Northwest Coast from the interior of North America. Equally importantly, however, the *ukaz* of September 4, 1821, laid claim to large areas of the northeastern Asian coast, where the Tsar's government was eyeing expansion toward the Amur River.[195]

Glynn Barratt put it this way: "Since the fall of 1820, the authorities of Petropavlovsk and at Novo-Arkhangel'sk had been obliged, despite their wishes, to enforce an isolationist and even xenophobic policy whereby all foreign ships and traders were excluded from the [Russian American] Company's own settlements and waters. Semi-isolation from the outside world and periodic hunger in the settlements became inevitable."[196]

It took more than a year for Murav'ev's letter of January 21, 1821, to reach the headquarters of the Russian American Company in St. Petersburg and for the Board of Directors to draft its reply. Regarding Murav'ev's report on the *Pedler's* visit to Novo-Arkhangel'sk in 1820, the Board wrote to Murav'ev on February 28, 1822: "It is a pity that you had not yet been informed of the right which has been officially declared and announced in the Regulations which have been sent to you by the "Apollo"[197] of the Imperial navy; if you had received these Regulations earlier, you would, no doubt, have searched Pigott's [sic] ship. Don't let these impudent fellows off so easily in the future."[198]

But the Russian naval ship *Apollon*, which was sent to patrol the coast and enforce the *ukaz*, only reached Novo-Arkhangel'sk in October, 1822, two years after the *Pedler's* visit. The *Apollon* carried the orders that closed the Russian territories in eastern Siberia and North America to foreign trade. Of course, the enforcement of these orders resulted in a severe shortage of food in the Russian settlements.[199] Similarly, these edicts put Murav'ev in a

[195]Galbraith 1977:19—20; Wegner 1984:35—36; Barratt 1983:5—6.

[196]Barratt 1990:149.

[197]The sloop-of-war *Apollon*.

[198]Fur Seal Arbitration, p. 388.

[199]Schabelski 1826; Farris 1993:47.

very difficult position, and his only recourse—other than urgently to petition the Company for relief—was to send ships to Hawaii and California for supplies.[200]

The governments of the United States and Great Britain quickly protested Russia's unilateral closure of the coasts she claimed and the extension of her boundaries in the North Pacific—and Russia backed down, first, in 1824, in a convention with the United States[201] and soon thereafter, in 1825, with Great Britain. These conventions now fixed Russian America's southern boundary at 54°40′N (the southern tip of Prince of Wales Island) and her eastern boundary at the 141st meridian west of Greenwich, but they allowed Americans and Britons free access to the coast for navigation, fishing, and trade for a period of ten years.[202] Russia thus achieved a strategic victory in gaining formal recognition of her boundaries in North America, but in all practicality the advantage was lost.

No American trading voyages are known to have gone to the Bering Strait region for nearly thirty years after the *Pedler's* voyage. Although the imperial ukaz did not claim the coast of America north of Bering Strait, as we have seen, the Americans found that there simply was not enough trade at Bering Strait, in comparison with other opportunities, to justify the time and expense, and perhaps the danger, of the voyage.

Nevertheless, the closure of the coasts did not greatly affect the American traders. Some found profits in carrying supplies to Novo-Arkhangel'sk on Murav'ev's orders; others simply ignored the closure and continued their smuggling on the Northwest Coast. But it is indisputable that the hunting pressure caused by the fur trade had severely suppressed the sea otter population, making profits more difficult to come by. Although new opportunities for trade arose on the coast of the Californias, at the same time Hawaii's sandalwood supply began to run low. By about 1825 John Jacob Astor, suffering ill health, essentially withdrew from the Pacific trade.

[200]Khlebnikov 1976:59; Pierce 1986:7—8; Barratt 1981:223.

[201]Walker 1999:81.

[202]Bancroft 1886:536—545; International Boundary Commission [1918]:202—211.

His trade with the United States' ports was by then far more important.[203]

For the Russians, and for the naval explorers Vasil'ev and Shishmarev, the voyage of the *Otkrytie* and *Blagonamerennyi* was not considered to have been a success because it produced only minor discoveries beyond those which Captain Cook had achieved. This may explain why no detailed account of their expedition was published in their lifetimes.[204] Count Rumiantsev, however, continued in his desire to expand on the discoveries he had sponsored via Kotzebue's voyage. He proposed to Murav'ev that the Russian American Company should join with him in underwriting the expense of another expedition.

Rumiantsev knew that the British Admiralty, as a response to the Russian expeditions, was sending Captain John Franklin to descend the Mackenzie River and to proceed west along the Arctic coast. Franklin was to rendezvous with a British naval vessel in Kotzebue Sound. Rumiantsev saw the advantage of having Russian explorers meet Franklin's expedition in northern Alaska, and he planned that this new Russian expedition should follow the American coast as far as the Mackenzie River. "If Russia should undertake nothing," he wrote to Murav'ev, "and the English should succeed in reaching Bering Strait, then the short distance of these regions from our Asiatic and American possessions will give Europe the right to reproach us for leaving such pursuits, in our own waters and around our shores, to other nations."

The expedition might have been important and productive, but, unfortunately for the Russians, Rumiantsev died in 1826, and his heir would not authorize the expenditure for the project, which in any case would have begun too late to meet Franklin.[205]

The next foreign exploration of the Bering Strait region and northern Alaska was Frederick William Beechey's voyage aboard HMS *Blossom* in 1826 and 1827. Beechey's highly successful expedition was sent to meet

[203]Porter 1931:672, 669—670.
[204]Ray 1983:2.
[205]Tikhmenev 1978:178; Kusov 1993.

John Franklin in Kotzebue Sound. But that rendezvous never occurred because in 1826 Franklin was stopped by ice on the north coast of Alaska, forcing his return to the Mackenzie.[206]

The *Kaŋiġmiut*—the Buckland River Eskimos—no doubt were emboldened by the success they believed they had achieved in 1820 through bullying the men from the *Blagonamerennyi.* Seven years later, however, when they used similar tactics to threaten a party from HMS *Blossom*, the British responded with gunfire to a volley of arrows, resulting in the death of one of the Eskimos. This encounter was the first recorded killing in northwestern Alaska between Eskimos and Europeans.[207]

But that day in the summer of 1820—when the *Pedler* lay at anchor in company with the Russian ships in Kotzebue Sound—was a unique moment in the history of the Bering Strait region. Trade and exploration had drawn men of three nations into contact. Russians, Americans, and *Kaŋiġmiut* encountered one another, and a vigorous maritime trade would develop in the Bering Strait region, a trade that the Americans had initiated, that the Russians would expand in the 1830s and 1840s, and that the Americans would dominate in the second half of the nineteenth century and thereafter.

[206]Beechey 1831; Peard 1973; Bockstoce 1977:9—17.

[207]Bockstoce 1977:129—132.

Bibliography

Armstrong, Terence

1965, *Russian Settlement in the North,* Cambridge; Cambridge University Press.

1994, Russian penetration into Siberia up to 1800, in P. E. H. Hair, *The European Outthrust and Encounter. The First Phase c. 1400–c. 1700: Essays in Tribute to David Beers Quinn on his 85th Birthday,* (ed.), Cecil H. Clough and Liverpool; Liverpool University Press, Liverpool Historical Studies, no. 12.

Bancroft, Hubert Howe

1886, *History of Alaska 1730–1885,* New York; Bancroft Company.

Barratt, Glynn

1981, *Russia in Pacific Waters, 1715–1825,* Vancouver and London; University of British Columbia Press.

1983, *Russian Shadows on the British Northwest Coast of North America, 1810–1890,* Vancouver; University of British Columbia Press.

1988, *The Russian View of Honolulu 1809–26,* Ottawa, Ontario; Carleton University Press.

1990, A note on trade between Oahu and the Russian Northwest Coast: 1806–1826, in *Russia in North America. Proceedings of the 2nd International Conference on Russian America,* Alaska History No. 35, Kingston, Ontario and Fairbanks, Alaska; Limestone Press, pp. 144–156.

Beechey, F.W.

1831 *Narrative of a Voyage to the Pacific and Beering's Strait, to Co-operate with the Polar Expeditions; Performed in His Majesty's Ship Blossom . . . in the Years* 1825, 26, 27, 28, London: Henry Colburn & Richard Bentley (2 vols).

Black, Lydia T.

2004, *Russians in Alaska, 1732–1867,* Fairbanks, Alaska; University of Alaska Press.

Bockstoce, John R.

1977, *Eskimos of Northwest Alaska in the Early Nineteenth Century,* Oxford; Pitt Rivers Museum, University of Oxford, Monograph 1.

1986, *Whales, Ice and Men. The History of Whaling in the Western Arctic,* Seattle; University of Washington Press.

1988 (ed.), *The Journal of Rochfort Maguire 1852–1854. Two Years at Point Barrow, Alaska, aboard H.M.S. "Plover" in the Search for Sir John Franklin,* London; Hakluyt Society (2 vols).

Bockstoce, John R. and Charles F. Batchelder

1978, A gazetteer of whalers' place-names for the Bering Strait region and the western Arctic, *Names. Journal of the American Name Society* 26, no. 3; 258–270.

Bogoras, W.

1904-1909. The Chukchee. *Memoirs of the American Museum of Natural History, 11.* New York: G. E. Stechert.

Burch, Ernest S., Jr.

1998a, *The Iñupiaq Eskimo Nations of Northwest Alaska,* Fairbanks; University of Alaska Press.

1998b, *International Affairs; The Cultural and Natural Heritage of Northwest Alaska (Vol. 7),* prepared for NANA Museum of the Arctic, Kotzebue, Alaska, and U. S. National Park Service, Anchorage, Alaska.

2003, *The Organization of National Life; The Cultural and Natural Heritage of Northwest Alaska (Vol. 6),* prepared for NANA Museum of the Arctic, Kotzebue, Alaska, and U. S. National Park Service, Anchorage, Alaska.

Chamisso, Adelbert von

1874, *Chamissos Werke,* (ed. Heinrich Kurz) Leipzig, Bibliographischen Instituts (2 vols).

1986, *A Voyage Around the World with the Romanzov Exploring Expedition in the Years 1815–1818 in the Brig "Rurik," Captain Otto von Kotzebue* (tr. and ed. Henry Kratz), Honolulu; University of Hawaii Press.

Choris, Louis

1822, *Voyage Pittoresque Autour du Monde, avec des Portraits de Sauvages d'Amerique, d'Asie, d'Afrique, et des Isles du Grand Ocean; des Paysages, des Vues Maritimes, et Plusieurs Objets D'Histoire Naturelle. . .*, Paris; Firmin Didot.

Cochrane, John Dundas

1824, *Narrative of a Pedestrian Journey Through Russia and Siberian Tartary, from the Frontiers of China to the Frozen Sea and Kamchatka,* London; Charles Knight, (2 vols).

Collier, Simon and William F. Sater

1996, *A History of Chile, 1808–1994,* Cambridge and New York; Cambridge University Press.

Cook, James and James King

1784, *A Voyage to the Pacific Ocean. . . 1776, 1777, 1778, 1779, 1780, 1784,* London; G. Nichol and T. Cadell (3 vols. and atlas).

Coxe, William

1780, *Account of the Russian Discoveries between Asia and America. To which Are Added, the Conquest of Siberia, and the History of the Transactions and Commerce Between Russia and China. . .*, London; T. Cadell.

Daws, Gavan

1968, *Shoal of Time. A History of the Hawaiian Islands,* Honolulu; University of Hawaii Press.

Dobell, Peter

1830, *Travels in Kamtchatka and Siberia; with a Narrative of a Residence in China,* London; Henry Colburn and Richard Bentley.

Dmytryshyn, Basil, E. A. P. Crownhart-Vaughan, and Thomas Vaughan

1989 *The Russian American Colonies 1798–1867 (To Siberia and Russian America. Three Centuries of Russian Eastward Expansion,* Vol. 3), North Pacific Studies Series, No. 11, Portland; Oregon Historical Society.

Efimov, A.V.

1964, *Atlas geograficheskikh otkrytii v Sibiri i severo-zapadnoi Amerike, XVII-XVIII vv* (Atlas of Geographic Discoveries in Siberia and Northwest America in the Seventeenth and Eighteenth Centuries), Moscow; Nauka.

Farris, Glenn

1993, The Russian Sloop "Apollo" in the North Pacific in 1822, *Sibirica* Vol. 1, no. 1; 47–70.

Fisher Raymond H.

1981, *The Voyage of Semen Dezhnev in 1648: Bering's Precursor,* London; The Hakluyt Society.

Fur Seal Arbitration

1895, *Proceedings of the Tribunal of Arbitration, convened at Paris under the treaty between the United States of America and Great Britain concluded at Washington February 20, 1892, for the determination of questions between the two governments concerning the jurisdictional rights of the United States in the waters of the Bering Sea,* Vol. VIII, Washington, DC: Government Printing Office.

Galbraith, John S.

1977, *The Hudson's Bay Company as an Imperial Factor 1821–1869,* New York; Octagon Books.

Gibson, James R.

1969, *Feeding the Russian Fur Trade. Provisionment of the Okhotsk Seaboard and the Kamchatka Peninsula 1639–1856,* Madison; University of Wisconsin Press.

1976, *Imperial Russia in Frontier America. The Changing Geography of Supply of Russian America, 1784–1867,* New York; Oxford University Press.

1991, Tsarist Russia in colonial America: Critical constraints, in *The History of Siberia from Russian Conquest to Revolution* (ed. Alan Wood). London and New York; Routledge.

1992, *Otter Skins, Boston Ships, and China Goods: the Maritime Fur Trade of the Northwest Coast, 1785–1841,* Montreal; McGill-Queen's University Press.

Gillesem, Karl Karlovich

1849, Puteshestvie na shliuppe *"Blagonamerennyi"* dlia issledovaniia beregov Azii I Ameriki za Beringovym prolivom s 1819 po 1822 god (The Voyage of the Sloop "Good Intent" to Investigate the Shores of Asia and America beyond Bering Strait, from 1819 to 1822), *Otechestvennye Zapiski* 55, no. 10; 67, no. 11; 67, no. 12; St. Petersburg.

1971, *(Karl K.) Hillsen's Journal, "Journey of the sloop 'Good Intent' to explore the Asiatic and American shores of Bering Strait, 1819 to 1822"* (ed. Dorothy Jean Ray and tr. Rhea Josephson), Typescript, Special Collections Department, Dartmouth College Library, Hanover, New Hampshire.

Golder, Frank A.

1917, *Guide to Materials for American History in Russian Archives,* Washington, DC; Carnegie Institution of Washington.

Gough, Barry M.

1986, British-Russian rivalry and the search for the Northwest Passage in the early 19th century, *Polar Record* 23, no. 144; 301–317.

Grimes, Eliab

MS. 1815–1825 Business Letter Book, M-459, Hawai'i State Archives, Honolulu.

Hayes, Derek

2001, *Historical Atlas of the North Pacific Ocean: Maps of Discovery and Scientific Exploration, 1500–2000,* Seattle, Washington; Sasquatch Books.

Holland, Clive

1994, *Arctic Exploration and Development c. 500 B.C. to 1915.* An Encyclopedia, New York and London; Garland Publishing.

Howay, F. W.

1973, *A List of Trading Vessels in the Maritime Fur Trade, 1785–1825,* Materials for the Study of Alaskan History, no. 2, Kingston, Ontario; Limestone Press

Hughes, Charles C.

1984, Siberian Eskimo, *Handbook of North American Indians, Vol. 5, Arctic,* Washington, DC; Smithsonian Institution; pp. 247–261.

Hultén, Eric

1968, *Flora of Alaska and Neighboring Territories. A Manual of the Vascular Plants,* Stanford, California; Stanford University Press.

International Boundary Commission

(1918), *Joint Report Upon the Survey and Demarcation of the International Boundary Between the United States and Canada Along the 141st Meridian. . .,* Washington, DC; U.S. Government Printing Office.

Johnson, Paul

1997 *A History of the American People,* New York; HarperCollins.

Khlebnikov, Kyrill T.

1976, *Colonial Russian America. Kyrill T. Khlebnikov's Reports, 1817–1832* (tr. and ed. Basil Dmytryshyn, and E. A. P. Crownhart-Vaughan), Portland, Oregon; Oregon Historical Society.

Khramchenko, [Khromchenko], V. S.

MS. *Zhurnal vedenyi na brige* "Golovnine" *v 1822m godu flota michmanom Khramchenko* (Journal kept on the brig "Golovnin" in 1822 by naval midshipman Khramchenko), Microfilm reel 2, item 12, Shur collection, Alaska and Polar Regions Department, Rasmuson Library, University of Alaska, Fairbanks. Original in State Archives of Perm Oblast', Russia, fond 445, opis' 1 ed. Khr. 74.

1973, V. S. Khromchenko's Coastal Explorations in Southwestern Alaska, 1822 (ed. James W. VanStone, tr. David H. Krauss), *Fieldiana Anthropology,* vol. 64.

Kotzebue, Otto von

1821a, *Entdeckungs-Reise in die Sud-See und nach der Berings-Strasse zur Erforschung einer nordöstlichen Durchfahrt. Unternommen in den Jahren 1815, 1816, 1817, und 1818. . . Grafen Rumanzoff auf dem Schiffe Rurick . . .*, Weimar; Gebrüdern Hoffman.

1821b, *A Voyage of Discovery, into the South Sea and Beering's Straits, for the Purpose of Exploring a North-East Passage, Undertaken in the Years 1815–1818. . .Count Romanzoff, in the Ship "Rurick". . .* , London; Longman, Hurst, Rees, Orme and Brown (3 vol).

Kusov, Vladimir Svyatoslavovich

1993, Count Nikolai Rumiantsev and Russian Exploration of Alaska and North America, *WAML Information Bulletin* 25, no. 1, (November): 11–22.

Lantzeff, George V. and Richard A. Pierce

1973, *Eastward to Empire: Exploration and Conquest on the Russian Open Frontier, to 1750,* Montreal and London; McGill-Queens University Press.

Lazarev, Aleksei Petrovich

1950, *Zapiski o plavanii voennogo shliupa Blagonamerennogo v Beringov proliv i vokrug sveta dlia otkrytii v 1819, 1820, 1821 i 1822 godakh* (Notes on the voyage of the naval sloop "Blagonamerennyi" in Bering Strait and round the world for discoveries in 1819, 1820, 1821 and 1822) (ed. A. I. Solov'ev), Moscow; Gosudarstvennoe Izdatel'stvo Geografischeskoi Literatury.

Ledyard, John

1783, *A Journal of Captain Cook's Last Voyage to the Pacific Ocean, and in Quest of a Northwest Passage, Performed in the Years 1776–79,* Hartford; Nathaniel Patten.

Lower, J. Arthur

1978, *Ocean of Destiny. A Concise History of the North Pacific, 1500–1978,* Vancouver; Univeristy of British Columbia Press.

Lütké, Fedor Petrovich

1835, *Voyage autour du monde, execute par ordre de Sa Majesté L'empereur Nicolas Ier, sur la corvette le Seniavine, dans les années 1826, 1827, 1828 et 1829, par Frédéric Lutké. . .*, Paris; Firmin Didot (3 vols and atlas).

Malloy, Mary

1998, *"Boston Men" on the Northwest Coast: The American Maritime Fur Trade 1788–1844,* Alaska History no. 47, Fairbanks, Alaska, and Kingston, Ontario; Limestone Press.

Masterson, James R. and Helen Brower

1948, *Bering's Successors 1745–1780. Contributions of Peter Simon Pallas to the History of Russian Exploration Toward Alaska,* Seattle; University of Washington Press.

Miller, Polly G.

1994, *Early Contact Glass Trade Beads in Alaska,* Altamonte Springs, Florida; Bead Society of Central Florida.

Ogden, Adele

1941, *The California Sea Otter Trade 1784–1848,* University of California Publications in History, Vol. 26, Berkeley and Los Angeles; University of California Press.

Orth, Donald J.

1967, *Dictionary of Alaska Place Names,* U. S. Geological Survey Professional Paper 567, Washington, DC; U. S. Government Printing Office.

Peard, George

1973, *To the Pacific and Arctic with Beechey. The Journal of Lieutenant George Peard of H.M.S. "Blossom" 1825–1828* (ed. Barry M. Gough), Cambridge; The Hakluyt Society.

Pierce, Richard A.

1965, *Russia's Hawaiian Adventure, 1815–1817,* Berkeley and Los Angeles; University of California Press.

1986 *Builders of Alaska. The Russian Governors 1818–1867;* Alaska History no. 28, Kingston, Ontario; Limestone Press.

1990, *Russian America: A Biographical Dictionary,* Alaska History no. 33, Kingston Ontario, and Fairbanks, Alaska; Limestone Press.

Porter, Kenneth Wiggins

1930, Cruise of Astor's brig Pedler, 1813–1816, *Oregon Historical Quarterly* 31, no. 3; 223–230.

1931, *John Jacob Astor: Business Man,* Cambridge, Massachusetts; Harvard University Press (2 vols).

1932, The cruise of the "Forester," *Washington Historical Quarterly 23,* 261–285.

Raeff, Marc

1956 *Siberia and the Reforms of 1822,* Seattle; University of Washington Press.

Ray, Dorothy Jean

1964, Nineteenth century settlements and settlement patterns in Bering Strait, *Arctic Anthropology* 2, no. 2, 61–94.

1975, Early maritime trade with the Eskimo of Bering Strait and the introduction of firearms, *Arctic Anthropology,* 12, no. 1: 1–9.

1983, *Ethnohistory in the Arctic. The Bering Strait Eskimo,* Alaska History, No. 23, Kingston, Ontario; The Limestone Press.

1992, *The Eskimos of Bering Strait,* 1650–1898, Seattle and London; University of Washington Press.

Ray, Dorothy Jean (ed.) and Rhea Josephson (tr.)

1971, *[Karl K.] Hillsen's Journal, "Journey of the sloop 'Good Intent' to explore the Asiatic and American shores of Bering Strait, 1819 to 1822,"* Typescript, Special Collections Department, Dartmouth College Library, Hanover, New Hampshire.

Sarychev, Gavril Andreevich

1806–1807 *Account of a Voyage of Discovery to the North-East of Siberia, the Frozen Ocean, and the North-East Sea,* London; Richard Phillips and J. G. Barnard.

Schabelski, Achille

1826, *Voyage aux Colonies Russes de l'Amerique, Fait à Bord du Sloop de Guerre, l'Apollon, Pendant les Années 1821, 1822, et 1823,* St. Petersburg; N. Gretsch.

Schweitzer, Peter P. and Evgeniy Golovko

1995, *Contacts Across Bering Strait, 1898–1948,* Report prepared for the U.S. National Park Service, Alaska Regional Office, December.

Shishmarev, Nikolai Dmitrievich

MS. *Travel notes kept aboard the sloop "Blagonamerennyi" during the round-the-world voyage in 1819–1821,* Russian State Naval Archive [RGAVMF]. F. 203, op. 1, d. 730[b], and microfilm copy, Shur Collection. Alaska and Polar Regions Department, Rasmuson Library, University of Alaska, Fairbanks.

Tikhmenev, P. A.

1978, *A History of the Russian-American Company* (tr. and ed. Richard A. Pierce and Alton S. Donnelly), Seattle and London; University of Washington Press.

Vagin, V. (comp.)

1872, *Istoricheskiia svedeniia o deiatel'nosti grafa M. M. Speranskago v Sibiri s 1819 po 1822 god* (Historical information on the activities of Count M. M. Speranskii in Siberia from 1819 to 1822), St. Petersburg (2 vols).

VanStone, James W.

1984, Mainland Southwest Alaska Eskimo, *Handbook of North American Indians, Vol. 5, Arctic,* Washington, DC; Smithsonian Institution; pp. 224–242.

Walker, James V.

1999, Mapping of the northwest boundary of the United States, 1800–1846: An historical context, *Terrae Incognitae 31,* 70–90.

Walters, John

MS. Diary of John Walters, Archival Manuscript Group #425, Historical Society of Dauphin County, Harrisburg, Pennsylvania.

Wenger, Donald B.

1984, *Russian-American Relations in Northeast Asia during the Nineteenth Century,* Doctoral Dissertation, Williamsburg, Virginia, Department of History, College of William and Mary.

Wolfe, James

MS. *Journal of a Voyage on Discovery in the Pacific and Beering's Straits on Board H.M.S. "Blossom" Capt. F. W. Beechey,* Beinecke Rare Book and Manuscript Library, Yale University, New Haven, Connecticut.

Index